Nͬgũgĩ wa Thiong'o was born in Limuru, Kenya, in 1938. He was educated at the Alliance High School, Kĩkũyũ, at Makerere University, Uganda and at the University of Leeds.

His novel, *Weep Not, Child,* was published in 1964 and this was followed by *The River Between* (1965), *A Grain of Wheat* (1967) and *Petals of Blood* (1977). *Devil on the Cross* (1980) was conceived and written during the author's one-year detention in prison, in Kenya, where he was held without trial after the performance by peasants and workers of his play *Ngaahika Ndeenda* (*I Will Marry When I Want*). This was his first work to be published in his own language, Gĩkũyũ, and then translated into English and many other languages. His novel *Matigari* was published in Gĩkũyũ in Kenya in 1986 and translated into English for the *African Writers Series* in 1989. The author has also written collections of short stories, plays and numerous essays.

Ngũgĩ is an active campaigner for the African language and form, and he writes, travels and lectures extensively on this theme. His work is known throughout the world and has made a powerful impact both at home and overseas.

NGŨGĨ WA THIONG'O

# THE RIVER BETWEEN

**HEINEMANN**

Heinemann is an imprint of Pearson Education Limited,
a company incorporated in England and Wales, having its
registered office at Edinburgh Gate, Harlow, Essex, CM20 2JE.
Registered company number: 872828

Heinemann is the registered trademark of Pearson Education Limited

Heinemann Publishers (Pty) Limited
PO Box 781940, Sandton 2146, Johannesburg, South Africa

British Library Cataloguing in Publication Data
A catalogue record for this book is available from the British Library.

AFRICAN WRITERS SERIES
and their accompanying logos are trademarks in the
United States of America of Heinemann:
A Division of Reed Publishing (USA) Inc.

ISBN: 978 0 435905 48 4

Printed in Malaysia (CTP-VVP)

20 19 18 17 16
IMP 50 49 48 47

In *The River Between*
the form of Gikuyu is
used correctly for
the people and
language of the Kikuyu area.

# CHAPTER ONE

The two ridges lay side by side. One was Kameno, the other was Makuyu. Between them was a valley. It was called the valley of life. Behind Kameno and Makuyu were many more valleys and ridges, lying without any discernible plan. They were like many sleeping lions which never woke. They just slept, the big deep sleep of their Creator.

A river flowed through the valley of life. If there had been no bush and no forest trees covering the slopes, you could have seen the river when you stood on top of either Kameno or Makuyu. Now you had to come down. Even then you could not see the whole extent of the river as it gracefully, and without any apparent haste, wound its way down the valley, like a snake. The river was called Honia, which meant cure, or bring-back-to-life. Honia river never dried: it seemed to possess a strong will to live, scorning droughts and weather changes. And it went on in the same way, never hurrying, never hesitating. People saw this and were happy.

Honia was the soul of Kameno and Makuyu. It joined them. And men, cattle, wild beasts and trees, were all united by this life-stream.

When you stood in the valley, the two ridges ceased to be sleeping lions united by their common source of life. They became antagonists. You could tell this, not by anything tangible but by the way they faced each other, like two rivals ready to come to blows in a life and death struggle for the leadership of this isolated region.

It began long ago. A man rose in Makuyu. He claimed that Gikuyu and Mumbi sojourned there with Murungu on their way to Mukuruwe wa Gathanga. As a result of that stay, he said, leadership had been left to Makuyu. Not all the

1

people believed him. For had it not always been whispered and rumoured that Gikuyu and Mumbi had stopped at Kameno? And had not a small hill grown out of the soil on which they stood south of Kameno? And Murungu had told them:

'This land I give to you, O man and woman. It is yours to rule and till, you and your posterity.'

The land was fertile. It was the whole of Gikuyu country from one horizon embracing the heavens to the other hidden in the clouds. So the story ran in Kameno. Spiritual superiority and leadership had then been left there.

Kameno had a good record to bear out this story. A sacred grove had sprung out of the place where Gikuyu and Mumbi stood; people still paid homage to it. It could also be seen, by any who cared to count, that Kameno threw up more heroes and leaders than any other ridge. Mugo wa Kibiro, that great Gikuyu seer of old, had been born there. And he had grown up, seeing visions of the future and speaking them to the many people who came to see and hear him. But a few, more cynical than their neighbours, would not go to him. They called him an impostor. Then one night, when people were asleep, he vanished from the hills. He was soon heard of in the land beyond; in Nyeri, Kiambu, Muranga; in fact all over the Gikuyu country. And he still spoke aloud his message and cried:

'There shall come a people with clothes like butterflies.'

These were the white men.

Or there was that great witch, Kamiri, whose witchery bewildered even the white men at Muranga. His witchery and magic, before he was overcome by the white men with smiles and gifts, had won him resounding fame. He too, it was said, had been born at Kameno. Like Mugo before him, he had disappeared from the hills to the country beyond. He could not be contained by the narrow life of the ridges.

Another was Wachiori, a great warrior, who had led the whole tribe against Ukabi, Masai. As a young man he had killed a lion, by himself. When he died, at the hands of a stray-

2

ing white man, he left a great name, the idol of many a young warrior.

The ridges were isolated. The people there led a life of their own, undisturbed by what happened outside or beyond. Men and women had nothing to fear. The Ukabi would never come here. They would be lost in the hills and the ridges and the valleys. Even other Gikuyu from Nyeri or Kiambu could not very well find their way into the hills. And so the country of many ridges was left alone, unaffected by turbulent forces outside. These ancient hills and ridges were the heart and soul of the land. They kept the tribes' magic and rituals, pure and intact. Their people rejoiced together, giving one another the blood and warmth of their laughter. Sometimes they fought. But that was amongst themselves and no outsider need ever know. To the stranger, they kept dumb, breathing none of the secrets of which they were the guardians. *Kagutui ka Mucii gatihakagwo Ageni*; the oilskin of the house is not for rubbing into the skin of strangers.

Leaders of the land rose from there. For though the ridges were isolated, a few people went out. These, who had the courage to look beyond their present content to a life and land beyond, were the select few sent by Murungu to save a people in their hour of need: Mugo, the great seer; Wachiori, the glorious warrior; Kamiri, the powerful magician.

They became strangers to the hills. Thereafter, the oilskin of the house was not for them. It was for those who lived inside. These were the people whose blood and bones spoke the language of the hills. The trees listened, moaned with the wind and kept silent. Bird and beast heard and quietly listened. Only sometimes they would give a rejoinder, joyful applause or an angry roar.

# CHAPTER TWO

The hills and the ridges now lay behind. This was a plain, the only such level stretch of land in this country. If you strained your eyes and peered into the misty distance you could see the land of Ukabi. It was all peaceful on this plain, which was said to have been a field of battle, once long ago. A few cattle pulled and mauled the grass while others lay down looking vacantly into space, chewing.

Suddenly, two boys emerged from the bush. They began to fight. One was tall and his unusually long neck and limbs made him appear older than he really was. He was Kamau, son of Kabonyi from Makuyu. The other, Kinuthia, was shorter with surprisingly strong muscles. His slow wide eyes well matched his smooth forehead. He lived with his uncle at a village beyond the two ridges away from Makuyu. His father had died early.

At first the boys fought with the sticks they had gone to fetch from the bush. The green sticks caught each other in mid-air several times and were soon in pieces. The boys threw them away and one piece touched a cow, which stood up quickly, frightened. It moved a few paces from the struggling pair, waking two others on the way. Then it looked in the opposite direction, unconcerned with the fight.

Kamau and Kinuthia were now wrestling. Their arms were interlocked and the two boys went round and round without either getting the better of the other. Kinuthia tried to lift Kamau off the ground and then trap him with his right leg. The attempt always failed. Kamau had his struggles too. Though not usually voluble, today he was eloquent with threats.

'You will know who I am,' he warned, at the same time using his right knee to hit Kinuthia's stomach.

'Cow,' cried Kinuthia with pain.

4

'Hyena.'

'Even you,' Kinuthia hissed back.

Kinuthia appeared much more collected, and an observer would have thought that he would win. But he tripped over a sharp stone and soon was lying prostrate on his stomach. Kamau bent over him and pinned Kinuthia's hands behind his head. His face was grim and contorted as he used his head to dig into Kinuthia's face, making his nose bleed. The boy underneath Kamau's knees felt pain. He thrust his legs in the air hoping to catch Kamau by the neck between the legs. Blows fell on him and he was bewildered, not knowing when and where the next blow would follow.

Two cows that had moved away together turned their heads and watched the struggle for a while. Then they bent their heads, thrusting out their tongues to pull and maul the grass like the others.

Just then, another boy came running from a group of cows a distance away.

'Stop fighting!' he shouted breathlessly as he stood near the pair. Kamau stopped, but he still sat on Kinuthia.

'Why are you fighting?'

'He called me names,' answered Kamau.

'He is a liar. He laughed at me because my father died poor and . . .'

'He called my father a convert to the white man.'

'He is!'

'You beggar.'

'White man's slave.'

'You . . . you . . .'

Kamau became furious. He began to pinch Kinuthia. Kinuthia looked appealingly to the other boy.

'Please stop this, Kamau. Didn't we swear that we of the hills were comrades?' He felt helpless. It was three days earlier that they had sworn to be brothers.

'What do I care about comrades who insult my father?' asked Kamau.

'I will do it again,' retorted Kinuthia between tears.

5

'Do now.'

'I will.'

'Try!'

Kamau and Kinuthia began to struggle. The boy felt an irre-
sistible urge to fall on Kamau; he pulled a blade of grass and
began to chew it quickly, his eyes dilating with rage and fear.

'Kamau,' he burst out.

The tremor in the boy's voice sent a quiver of fear up
Kamau. He quickly looked up and met the burning eyes, gazing
at him. Meekly he obeyed the unspoken command. But his face
went a shade darker than it normally was. He slunk away, feeling humiliated and hating himself for submitting. Kinuthia
stood up unsteadily and looked gratefully at the boy. The boy
kept on lowering his face, gazing at the same spot. The feeling
of pride and triumph he had suddenly felt at seeing Kamau
obey him had as suddenly subsided to one of regret at having
done that to him. Perhaps it might have felt better if Kamau
had stuck it out and he had had to use force to remove him.

The boy's name was Waiyaki, the only son of Chege. He was
quite young; not of Kamau or Kinuthia's age. He had not even
gone through his second birth. Waiyaki was, however, already
tall for his age. He had a well-built, athletic body. His hair
was tough and dry with kinks that finished in a clear outline on
the forehead. Just above the left eye was a slightly curved scar.
He had got it from a wild goat. The goat had run after one of
the herdboys. Seeing this, Waiyaki had taken a stick and run
after the goat shouting. The goat turned on him and jabbed
him with its horns, tearing the flesh to the bone. His father
arrived in time to save him. That was a long while ago. The
wound had healed, leaving him a hero among the boys although he had run after the goat for sheer fun and enjoyment
of the scene. That, however, was not the sole reason why the
other boys, young and old, promptly followed him.

Chege, his father, was a well-known elder in Kameno. He
had now only one wife, who had borne him many daughters
but only one son. The other two wives had died during the

great famine, without any children. The famine had been preceded by a very rich harvest. Then locusts and worms and a long drought came to bring death to many. Chege had barely survived. His daughters were now well married, apart from one, who had died early. The other elders feared and respected him. For he knew, more than any other person, the ways of the land and the hidden things of the tribe. He knew the meaning of every ritual and every sign. So, he was at the head of every important ceremony.

Many stories ran around him. Some people said that he had the gift of magic. Others said that he was a seer and Murungu often spoke to him. And so they said that he could see visions of the future like Mugo wa Kibiro, who a long time back prophesied the invasion of the Gikuyu country by the white man. Some even said that Chege was actually related to Mugo. Nobody knew this for sure. Chege himself claimed nothing. Ever since he had warned the people against Siriana Missionary Centre and they had refused to hear his voice, he had talked little, keeping all thoughts to himself. Chege had told the people of the ridges what had happened in Muranga, Nyeri and Kiambu. He told them of Tumu Tumu, Gikuyu, Limuru and Kijabe. They doubted his voice, saying:

'How do you know?'

'See them, the butterflies.'

'Butterflies? You have never left the ridges!'

'They are there, beyond the ridges, putting up many houses and some taking the land.'

'How could you have seen the light beyond?'

'Fools, fools,' he muttered to himself in despair.

Nairobi was already flourishing, and the railway was moving across the country in the land beyond where not many from the ridges had been. And they lowered their voices and whispered together:

'The white man cannot speak the language of the hills.'

'And knows not the ways of the land.'

But the white man had come to Siriana, and Joshua and Kabonyi had been converted. They had abandoned the ways of the ridges and followed the new faith. Still people shrugged their shoulders and went on with their work, whispering:

'Who from the outside can make his way into the hills?'

Chege had then been young. Now he was growing old. However, he remembered something in his old age. A light shone in his eyes, a flicker of hope. He would guard it and divulge the knowledge to none but the right one.

The boys did not want to be caught by the darkness. They collected their cattle together and drove them home. Many paths ran through the forest to various huts scattered over the ridges. Unless you were careful, you could easily lose your way in the hills; one part of the forest looked so much like another. But the boys, born and brought up in the hills, knew the paths.

Darkness was settling when Waiyaki reached home. Chege had been waiting for him. He called Waiyaki to his *thingira*, the man's hut. He sat on a stool, leaning against the central pole. A fire burnt low and, when Waiyaki entered and stood close to the door, Chege took a stick lying near him and poked the fire slowly. Sparks flew upwards in quick succession.

'Why do you come home with darkness?' Chege at last asked, without raising his head. He spat on the floor.

'We took the cattle to the plains.'

'The plains?'

'Yes, Father.'

After a small silence – 'That is far to go,' he said.

Waiyaki kept quiet. He was never at ease in front of his father.

'Danger lurks in darkness.'

'Yes, Father.'

Again Waiyaki was uneasy. He darted a quick glance at the door. His father had not yet looked up.

'Who showed you the way?'

'I know all the ways in the ridges,' he said proudly to impress the father he secretly feared. Besides this, Waiyaki did not like to be thought young for he considered himself able to make decisions like a man.

8

Chege looked at his son. He contemplated him for a while. Waiyaki tried to puzzle what his father was thinking. And suddenly it occurred to him that his father had been anxious and had feared for him. A feeling of pride warmed his heart and he wondered if the other boys could boast of such a father.

'You have not eaten.' There was softness in Chege's voice.

'I have just come.'

'Go then and get your mother to give you something to put in your mouth. You must be hungry.'

Waiyaki made to move. But as he was about to go out, his father called him back. Waiyaki now trembled a little.

'Remember, tomorrow is the day of your second birth.'

'Yes, Father.'

'Do not forget,' Chege said with an unnecessary emphasis.

Waiyaki ran to his mother's hut. How could he forget such an event?

# CHAPTER THREE

Demi na Mathathi were giants of the tribe. They had lived a long way back, at the beginning of time. They cut down trees and cleared the dense forests for cultivation. They owned many cattle, sheep and goats and they often sacrificed to Murungu and held communion with the ancestral spirits. Waiyaki had heard about these two generations of the tribe and he was proud of them. Only he wished he knew what they had looked like. They must have been great and strong to have braved the hazards of the forest.

Sometimes in the bush, he and the other boys played Demi na Mathathi. One day a boy from Koina told Waiyaki:

'You cannot be Demi.'

'Why?' he asked. The other boys came round.

'You are not ready for circumcision. You are not born again.'

Waiyaki looked at the ground and felt small. Then he turned to the group and let his eyes fall on them. His eyes were large and rather liquid; sad and contemplative. But whenever he looked at someone, they seemed to burn bright. A light came from them, a light that appeared to pierce your body, seeing something beyond you, into your heart. Not a man knew what language the eyes spoke. Only, if the boy gazed at you, you had to obey. That half-imploring, half-commanding look was insisting, demanding. Perhaps that was why the other boys obeyed him. His mother always turned her eyes away from his. And some women and big girls remarked that he made them feel shy. But then women were always shy when men's eyes were on them. Waiyaki was not aware of anything strange in his eyes, although sometimes he felt something burn in him, urging him to say and do daring things.

And that day he felt the urge come to him. For a moment he thought himself Demi as he answered back.

'But I am Demi.' And then he saw a tree a little distance away. 'See if I don't cut down that tree,' he went on. And he took an axe and rushed to the tree, oblivious of everything. He began to cut it with all his strength and soon the stick that was the axe fell into pieces. At first the other boys had laughed. But they soon followed his example and went around cutting down trees and clearing the forest ready for 'Cultivation' just like Demi na Mathathi.

That day Waiyaki went home and told his mother: 'I must be born again.'

Now the day had come. And when the sun rose and hit the ground and goats scratched themselves against the wall, Waiyaki went to the back of the hut and let the rays fall on his neck. The burning was pleasant.

Waiyaki wanted to be happy, very happy. Was he not going to learn the ways of the land? Was he not going to drink the magic ritual of being born again? He knew he wanted to be like his father, knowing all the ways of the land from Agu and Agu, long ago.

But he felt dejected. Something he could not define seemed to gnaw at his soul, having first crept through the flesh. He wished Kamau or Kinuthia were there to keep him company. And yet he had wanted this thing. As the sun shone on his skin, he held his muscles taut and shut his eyes, trying to recapture the feeling of importance he had experienced in the days of waiting. The anticipation had been sweet. Now it did not matter. Only after today he would be ready for the biggest of all rituals, circumcision. This would mark his final initiation into manhood. Then he would prove his courage, his manly spirit.

Much beer had been brewed and many elders were beginning to arrive. Two had come early in the morning and were now busy slaughtering a goat. Everyone who was present would eat meat. And the spirits of the dead and the living would be invoked to join in the ritual.

The ceremony did not take long. It was not even complicated. His mother sat near the fireplace in her hut as if in labour. Waiyaki sat between her thighs. A thin cord taken from the slaughtered goat and tied to his mother represented the umbilical cord. A woman, old enough to be a midwife, came and cut the cord. The child began to cry. And the women who had come to wait for the birth of a child, shouted with joy:

> 'ali-li-li-li-li-li-lii
> Old Waiyaki is born
> Born again to carry on the ancient fire.'

For a time, Waiyaki forgot himself and thought he was Demi, bravely clearing the forest, a whole tribe behind him. But when he looked around and saw old women surrounding him, he began to cry again like a little child. He felt the pain of fear inside himself. He tried to open his eyes wide, wide, and for a moment he had a flashing maddening sensation that they would not open. He trembled and thought himself shrinking with cold. He had never felt this before and tears continued flowing, falling to the ground. The women went on shouting but Waiyaki did not see them now. Their voices were a distant buzz like another he had heard in a dream when a swarm of bees came to attack him. He cried the more. People became frightened. This was not what usually happened.

Later in the day, his mother went into the field. Waiyaki, whose head had been shorn of hair, trailed behind her as a little child would follow its mother. And when she went to Honia river, he followed. She dipped him into the water and he came out clean.

He went to bed early. A strange hollowness settled in his stomach. The whole thing had been a strange experience. He was glad that the ceremony was over. But somewhere a glow of pride was beginning. He was ready for initiation.

# CHAPTER FOUR

Soon Waiyaki joined again in the daily rhythm of life in the village. He went out to look after cattle; organized raids, went out hunting. He joined in the dances for the young boys and felt happy. Days came and went; and still it was the same life. His eyes retained a strong and resolute look. Some people said that there was something evil in their glitter. But his father must have had the same sort of eyes; in a body becoming distorted with wrinkles, his eyes remained alive and youthful.

One evening, a few weeks after his second birth, Waiyaki was called by his father, who liked holding talks in his *thingira*, the man's hut. Waiyaki entered very quietly, because he was always uneasy in the presence of his father.

Chege was sitting in his usual place by the pole. Goats and sheep slept together around him and a low snore came from them.

'Sit down,' Chege said, and indicated a small, four-legged stool standing legs upwards near a fat sheep which slept very close to the fireplace. Waiyaki poked the sheep in the ribs with the left leg so that he might get a place to sit. The sheep would not move and Waiyaki was forced to sit next to it. 'Where do you take the cattle tomorrow?'

'The Valley in Nyama!'

'Have you been to the hills deep south of Kameno?' Chege spoke slowly. Except for a slight tremor in the voice, it was young and calm.

'No!' Waiyaki answered after a slight pause. He was trying to recall the place. He wondered why his father was asking him all this.

'Have you ever heard of the sacred grove?'

'Yes, we hear about it.'

There was another silence. Waiyaki grew restless with curiosity.

'Leave the cattle and goats with your mother, for tomorrow we shall go to the hills.'

Outside it was dark. A few stars lay scattered across the sky. Waiyaki was excited. He felt ready to start on the journey there and then. What were they going to do together, what were they going to see? It was a secret, a man's secret. What other hidden things did his father hold in his ageing body? He wished Chege had told him more, but he would know all, everything, tomorrow. It would be a great day. The journey was important. As he ran into his mother's hut and sat down, he felt important and very big.

Chege and Waiyaki trudged on. The path they followed was unknown to Waiyaki as he had never gone that far along Honia river. But he was content to follow his father, who led the way through the labyrinth of bush thorns and creeping plants. Waiyaki was often caught in the network of plants and thorns, sometimes extricating himself with difficulty.

Nothing stirred. Only the throb and fall of the river accompanied the occasional plash and slither of their footfalls. Sometimes Chege would stop and seem to listen. Waiyaki stopped too but would hear nothing. Chege would then pour a shower of saliva on to his breast in the Gikuyu way of blessing. Waiyaki thought his father was blessing the river.

Few words passed between them. But when Chege stopped near a certain tree or bush, Waiyaki knew that his father had something to explain.

'The bark of that tree is good for a fresh wound.'

'The roots of this plant are good. When your stomach bites you, you boil them in water. Drink the liquid.'

And sometimes it would be a warning against that tree, 'whose fruit is full of poison.'

Waiyaki felt close to his father as he had never felt before. He felt a glow rising inside him. Was he not drinking from a calabash of trust and responsibility? *Tiitheru*, of a truth, he was maturing. The hidden things of the hills were being revealed to him.

They left the valley and began to climb up the slopes, past a rock here or a tree there. Waiyaki was surprised at his father, who seemed to keep the same pace, while he himself was already panting. Once they disturbed an antelope from its hiding place. It leapt – leapt – leapt away. Waiyaki liked antelopes. He always felt a desire to touch their smooth bodies.

'They see men and run away.'

'Why? Don't they run away from women?' Waiyaki asked, puzzled. The forest was quiet. One could still catch the fading throb of the river.

'You don't know this! Long ago women used to rule this land and its men. They were harsh and men began to resent their hard hand. So when all the women were pregnant, men came together and overthrew them. Before this, women owned everything. The animal you saw was their goat. But because the women could not manage them, the goats ran away. They knew women to be weak. So why should they fear them?'

It was then Waiyaki understood why his mother owned nothing.

They came to the top. There, they found a beaten path which appeared to have been out of use for a long time. They took it. Ahead of them was a small hill standing all by itself. On top was the sacred place. Waiyaki's heart gave a jump. He felt afraid and excited at the same time.

A big Mugumo tree stood near the edge of the hill. It was a huge tree, thick and mysterious. Bush grew and bowed reverently around it. And there the ancient tree stood, towering over the hill, watching, as it were, the whole country. It looked holy and awesome, dominating Waiyaki's soul so that he felt very small and in the presence of a mighty power. This was a sacred tree. It was the tree of Murungu. Waiyaki, now on top of the hill, on the other side of the tree, surveyed the land. And he felt as if his heart would stop beating so overcome was he by the immensity of the land. The ridges were all flat below his small feet. To the east, the sun had already risen. It could now be seen clearly, a huge red ball of smouldering colours. Strands of yellowish-red thinned outwards from the glowing centre, diffusing into the thick grey that joined the land to the clouds. Far beyond, its tip hanging in the grey clouds, was Kerinyaga. Its snow-capped top glimmered slightly, revealing the seat of Murungu.

The ridges slept on. Kameno and Makuyu were no longer antagonistic. They had merged into one area of beautiful land, which is what, perhaps, they were meant to be. Makuyu, Kameno and the other ridges lay in peace and there was no sign of life, as one stood on the hill of God.

# CHAPTER FIVE

Even Chege was moved by the morning peace. It was sometime before he was able to speak.

'Do you see all this land, this country stretching beyond and joining the sky?' His voice was deep and calm. Waiyaki realized that it was charged with strong feelings. He whispered:

'Yes.'

'It is beautiful to the eye—'

'It is beautiful.'

'And young and fertile—'

'Yes. Young and fertile.'

'All this is our land.'

'Yes, Father.'

'You know Gikuyu and Mumbi—'

'Father and mother of the tribe.'

It was as if both were in a big dream.

'Do you see that mountain showing through the grey mist on the horizon—'

'Kerinyaga?'

'Yes, the mountain of He-who-shines-in-Holiness.' Chege stopped but continued with his steadfast look. 'That is the seat of Murungu. He made Gikuyu and Mumbi.'

'Ye-es.' Waiyaki whispered.

'He stood them on that mountain. He showed them all the land.'

'Ye-es.' Again it was a whisper, barely audible. His father's voice had a magic spell.

'From that mountain he brought them here.' Chege was standing beside his son, but a few steps behind. He looked across the ridges, across the hills, gazing still into space, like a man in a vision. Perhaps he was looking at something hidden from Waiyaki. Waiyaki strained his eyes but could not see anything. Although he feared for his father, he was becoming overpowered by the words flowing from the old man. And his father spoke on, not really talking to Waiyaki, but rather talking to himself, speaking his feelings and thoughts aloud. As his voice vibrated, Chege seemed to gain in stature and appearance so that Waiyaki thought him transfigured.

'... it was before Agu; in the beginning of things. Murungu brought the man and woman here and again showed them the whole vastness of the land. He gave the country to them and their children and the children of the children, *tene na tene*, world without end. Do you see here?'

Waiyaki was not sure if the last question was addressed to him. However, he looked up and saw his father was pointing at the Mugumo tree and the mysterious bush around it.

'That is a blessed and sacred place. There, where Mumbi's feet stood, grew up that tree. So you see, it is Kameno that supported the father and mother of the tribe. From here, Murungu took them and put them under Mukuruwe wa Gathanga in Muranga. There our father and mother had nine daughters who bore more children. The children spread all over the country. Some came to the ridges to keep and guard the ancient rites. . . .'

The old man shifted his gaze and looked at his son.

'You are here. . . .'

'I came with you, Father.' Waiyaki was puzzled. He was beginning to shake himself out of the powers of the spell.

'I know, I know,' he said impatiently. 'You understand that Gikuyu and Mumbi set their footsteps here.'

'Yes.'

'You descend from those few who came to the hills.'

There was a moment of silence between them. Waiyaki did not understand.

'You have heard of Mugo wa Kibiro?'

'Yes.'

'He was a seer ... he saw things ... the future unfolded before his eyes. . . .

'Mugo was born and grew up in Kameno before he went to

**18**

tell people what he saw. For he saw many butterflies, of many colours, flying about over the land, disrupting the peace and the ordered life of the country. Then he cried aloud and said: "There shall come a people with clothes like butterflies. ...." People did not believe him. Some even poured scorn on him, laughing at him, for they said: "He is not well." And they would not listen to his voice, which warned them: "Beware!" The seer was rejected by the people of the ridges. They gave him no clothes and no food. He became bitter and hid himself, refusing to tell them more. He went beyond the hills, to the world yonder, the whole extent of Gikuyuland. He was not yet exhausted and there spoke the message even louder. Still they laughed and poured scorn on him. Here they thought him dead. But disguised he came back here and settled.'

Chege paused for a while as if to gather his breath. His eyes shone as if with inner power and then slowly he said:

'We are his offspring. His blood flows in your veins.'

Waiyaki stood as if dumb. The knowledge that he had in him the blood of this famous seer, who had been able to see the future, filled him with an acute sense of wonder. He could not speak; the only word which escaped him was 'Ha!' His father was still speaking:

'He died here. Our fathers do not know where his grave is. But some say that he was carried up by Murungu.'

Chege stopped and slowly turned to Waiyaki. Waiyaki trembled freely.

'I see you fear. You must learn to fight fear ... fear. ... It was not only Mugo whom they rejected. When I told them about Siriana they would not listen.'

For the first time, Waiyaki felt really frightened. Unknown terror gripped him. He fought with it.

'No doubt you wonder why I tell you all this—'

Waiyaki wanted to cry out: 'Don't tell me more. I don't want to hear more. No! No! No, Father!' Instead he only whispered.

'Ye-es!'

'You are the last in our line.'

Waiyaki felt as if a heavy cloud was pressing down his soul and he felt a strange sensation of suspension in his stomach. It was as if something, a presentiment, was moving towards him with all speed and he was powerless to prevent it.

'Sit down,' his father spoke gently.

Waiyaki's legs had already begun to lose strength and he sank on to the grass.

'You are tired perhaps,' Chege said as he moved near his son.

Waiyaki stopped trembling and hated himself for showing fear.

Chege repeated slowly:

'You see, when Mugo became bitter, he refused to tell them more.' Chege made another pause. His face and eyes were set as if he was trying to recall something long-forgotten. . . . He was now standing just behind Waiyaki. He bent down and touched his son on the shoulder. Waiyaki realized that his father's hand was trembling slightly. Chege withdrew his hand quickly and then with a loud tremor in his voice went on:

'Now, listen my son. Listen carefully, for this is the ancient prophecy. . . . I could not do more. When the white man came and fixed himself in Siriana, I warned all the people. But they laughed at me. Maybe I was hasty. Perhaps I was not the one. Mugo often said you could not cut the butterflies with a panga. You could not spear them until you learnt and knew their ways and movement. Then you could trap, you could fight back. Before he died, he whispered to his son the prophecy, the ancient prophecy: "Salvation shall come from the hills. From the blood that flows in me, I say from the same tree, a son shall rise. And his duty shall be to lead and save the people!" He said no more. Few knew the prophecy. Perhaps Kabonyi, who has betrayed the tribe, knows about it. I am old, my time is gone. Remember that you are the last in this line.

'Arise. Heed the prophecy. Go to the Mission place. Learn all the wisdom and all the secrets of the white man. But do not follow his vices. Be true to your people and the ancient rites.'

20

'Father—' Waiyaki called out when he had recovered from the shock. He felt weak and small. He did not know what he wanted to say.

'You go there. I tell you again, learn all the wisdom of the white man. And keep on remembering, salvation shall come from the hills. A man must rise and save the people in their hour of need. He shall show them the way; he shall lead them.'

'But – but – they don't know me. I am a child and they rejected Mugo. . . .'

'Let them do what they like. A time will come – I can see it coming – when they shall cry for a saviour. . . .'

It was late in the day when Chege and Waiyaki descended the hills. They reached home both feeling exhausted. To Waiyaki the whole experience seemed a dream. What had he, a mere boy, to do with a saviour? Was he to go about in the ridges crying, 'Listen! A leader shall come from the hills to save you'?

And then for a time he began to doubt the sanity of his father. Perhaps the whole thing had been an old man's dream. He almost laughed at the serious manner in which his father had taken it all. But there was no mirth in his heart. Instead he felt a heaviness making him a man. In body, he was still a boy.

When the time came, Waiyaki vanished from the hills without the knowledge of any but his father. He went to Siriana, where, one term later, and almost by a miracle, he was joined by Kamau and Kinuthia, his fellow herdboys.

The three were destined to live and learn together under the Reverend Livingstone of Siriana Mission, which had now grown into a big institution. Many boys from the hills and beyond, from Kiambu and Muranga, came there for a portion of the white man's magic.

For many seasons they learned and worked hard. Waiyaki made quick progress and impressed the white missionaries, who saw in him a possible brave Christian leader of the Church. But who knew that things were changing faster than the vision of Livingstone, than the boy's expectation and imaginings?

# CHAPTER SIX

Mornings were normally chilly and cold in both Kameno and Makuyu. Nyambura felt the cold bite into her skin as she sat on her already full water-barrel. She looked fixedly at her young sister, who was still in the process of filling hers. Then she looked at the pale dark water of the river. It flowed on just as it had done for years, making incessant gurgling sounds as it made its way round the projecting rocks. Nyambura was fascinated and felt attracted to the river. Her breast, glowing with pleasure, rose and fell with a sigh: she felt something strange stirring in her bowels. It was an exhilaration, a feeling of acute ecstasy, almost of pain, which always came to her as she watched the snaky movement and listened to the throb of the river.

The importance of Honia could never be overestimated. Cattle, goats and people drew their water from there. Perhaps that was why it was called 'Cure' and the valley, the valley of life; that is what it was, a valley of life.

During the initiation ceremonies, boys and girls came to wet their bodies here on the morning of circumcision. It had long been discovered that very cold water numbed the skin, making it less painful during the operation. Nyambura thought of this and felt slightly guilty. She looked apprehensively at her sister, who was still drawing water. Nyambura wondered whether such thoughts ever came to Muthoni. She thought not and envied her. For Nyambura had learnt and knew that circumcision was sinful. It was a pagan rite from which she and her sister had been saved. A daughter of God should never let even a thought of circumcision come to her mind. Girls of their age would be initiated this season. Had her father, Joshua, not been a man of God, he, no doubt, would have presented them both as candidates.

'Nyambura, sister—'

Nyambura woke up from her wicked reverie. Her sister had spoken to her. Nyambura looked at her and wondered. What was worrying Muthoni? What was gnawing at the young girl's spirit? Nyambura was in no doubt that something was the matter with Muthoni. All through the week and in fact all through the last two months she had noticed something moody and restless in the young girl. This had pained Nyambura. She loved her sister.

Indeed, the two were inseparable. They played and worked together. Nyambura was older, but it was not easy to tell this. Both were fairly tall and well formed; about the same height and looks, though Muthoni's skin was darker. They had the same sharp but strangely restless eyes. Their hair was thick and shiny black. It was tough but to the eyes it looked soft and beautiful to touch.

Nyambura's features seemed hard, restrained. Where she was quiet, Muthoni was vivacious.

So it was not surprising that Nyambura should have noticed this sudden change of spirits. Coming to the river that morning Muthoni had been more withdrawn than ever before. Nyambura was deeply disturbed because her earlier attempts to coax her to reveal her troubles had failed. Now she waited for her to continue. Muthoni was sitting on her own water-barrel.

'I want to tell you something,' she said.

'Oh, please do,' Nyambura responded eagerly, her curiosity sharpened.

'But promise me that you will keep what I tell you to yourself.' This was an appeal, an appeal almost of fear. Nyambura would have laughed but for the earnestness in the voice and look of her sister.

'Well, first tell me about that something,' Nyambura said carelessly. She wanted to make her sister relax and soften the tense look on her face. Muthoni raised her face to Nyambura. This time the appeal was quite unmistakable.

'I have thought and thought again about it. I have not been

able to eat or sleep properly. My thoughts terrify me. But I think now I have come to a decision.' She stopped; gazing past Nyambura, she said, slowly and quietly:

'Nyambura, I want to be circumcised.'

For a second Nyambura sat as if her thoughts, her feelings, her very being had been paralysed. She could not speak. The announcement was too sudden and too stupefying. How could she believe what she had heard came from Muthoni's mouth? She looked at the river, at the slightly swaying bulrushes lining the banks, and then beyond. Nothing moved on the huge cattle road that wound through the forest towards Kameno. The yellowish streaks of morning light diffused through the forest, producing long shadows on the cattle path. The insects in the forest kept up an incessant sound which mingled with the noise of falling water farther down the valley. They helped to intensify the silence, created by Muthoni's statement.

'Circumcised?' At last Nyambura found her voice.

'Yes.'

'But Father will not allow it. He will be very cross with you. And how can you think of it?' Nyambura could visualize Joshua's fury if he heard of this.'Besides,' she continued, 'you are a Christian. You and I are now wise in the ways of the white people. Father has been teaching us what he learnt at Siriana. And you know, the missionaries do not like the circumcision of girls. Father has been saying so. Besides, Jesus told us it was wrong and sinful.'

'I know. But I want to be circumcised.'

'Why?' Nyambura asked helplessly.

She knew quite well that her father would not hear of such a thing. Every man of God knew that this was a pagan rite against which, time and time again, the white missionaries had warned Joshua. Perhaps Satan had gone into Muthoni. That was how the devil worked. Nyambura tried to reason with her sister.

'Yes. Tell me. Why do you want this? You know this is the devil's work. You know how he tempts people. You and I are

**25**

Christians. Were we not baptized long ago? Are you not now saved from sin?' Nyambura was becoming passionate. She breathed hard and she felt a warmth inside. She was defending something; she was trying to save her sister.

'I know but—' Muthoni paused. She had never seen her sister like that, with that light in her eyes. She felt weak in the knees and thought she was wrong. But the next moment she jumped up and rushed to her sister. She spoke earnestly and passionately. After all, she too believed in what she was going to do. Nyambura clasped her arms and they remained locked in each other's arms like little children. Nyambura became alarmed at the passion in Muthoni. She spoke gently:

'Father and Mother—'

'Look, please, I – I want to be a woman. I want to be a real girl, a real woman, knowing all the ways of the hills and ridges.'

'But Father, remember him.'

'Why! Are we fools?' She shook Nyambura. 'Father and mother are circumcised. Are they not Christians? Circumcision did not prevent them from being Christians. I too have embraced the white man's faith. However, I know it is beautiful, oh so beautiful to be initiated into womanhood. You learn the ways of the tribe. Yes, the white man's God does not quite satisfy me. I want, I need something more. My life and your life are here, in the hills, that you and I know.' She spoke now, looking beyond Nyambura as if to some other people. Then she lowered her voice and whispered secretly, 'Father said that at the Mission there is that man – Livingstone – and many women. Those are his wives. And do you think that he, a man, would marry a woman not circumcised? Surely there is no tribe that does not circumcise. Or how does a girl grow into a woman?' Muthoni had now released herself from the grasp. She now stood and looked away from Nyambura.

Nyambura could not say anything. She did not follow Muthoni's logic or line of thought. She had never thought so deeply about these things. She was content to follow whatever her father said was right. And she feared his anger. Muthoni

26

turned and again held her sister, appealing with her eyes and her body.

'Please, Sister. Don't tell. Don't tell Father.'

They both began to weep into one another. Nyambura's heart softened and she felt pity for her sister. She earnestly wished she could help her but felt her own powerlessness very acutely.

'How will you be initiated?'

'Father and Mother will not know. But I don't know where to go.'

'Our aunt lives at Kameno,' Nyambura tried to help.

'Oh, yes. I had thought of that. I will go to Kameno and stay with her when the season comes.'

What else could Nyambura do? She tried again to remonstrate with her sister, without any result. In her heart, she knew that once Muthoni had resolved on something it was difficult to make her change her mind. She had inherited this stubborn spirit from Joshua, a man who, once he made up his mind, was hard to deflect from his set purpose.

Honia river flowed on. The insects went on with their incessant sound mingling with the fall of the river. The whole scene became fearful to Nyambura and she no longer felt excited. Even the warmth of the morning sun did not awaken her. She loved her sister and now was troubled because she did not know what would happen.

They took their tin water-barrels and began the slow ascent of the ridge back to their home in Makuyu. Suddenly Nyambura heard a slight groan from her sister. She quickly turned round; a look of dismay was on Muthoni's face; her water-barrel was rolling down the slope back to the river.

Nyambura and Muthoni had to go down again. 'A bad omen,' Nyambura thought.

# CHAPTER SEVEN

The women and men of Makuyu were already up and about their morning chores by the time the two girls, with their water-barrels weighing heavily on their backs, reached home. All along the ridge, thick blue smoke was curling upwards, issuing from the scattered, mud-walled huts that made up the village. Some women, apparently not early risers, were just now going to the river to fetch water, while here and there, cattle and goats, with small boys trotting after them, trailed in all directions.

There was a general uniformity between all the houses that lay scattered over this ridge. They consisted of round thatched huts standing in groups of three or four. A natural hedge surrounded each household. Joshua's house was different. His was a tin-roofed rectangular building standing quite distinctly by itself on the ridge. The tin roof was already decaying and let in rain freely, so on top of the roof could be seen little scraps of sacking that covered the very bad parts. The building, standing so distinctly and defiantly, was perhaps an indication that the old isolation of Makuyu from the rest of the world was being broken down.

As yet, it was true, no town was near. Nairobi was far, a town not known to the hills. Siriana was still the nearest missionary centre: a big place with hospitals and a flourishing school taking boys and girls from all over the country. But the missionaries had not as yet penetrated into the hills, though they sent a number of disciples to work there. The people remained conservative, loyal to the ways of the land. Livingstone occasionally paid a visit to the hills, giving new life and energy to his various followers. His main work, however, was being carried on by Joshua.

Joshua, Nyambura's father, was now a middle-aged man

who always preached in sharp ringing tones that spoke of power and knowledge. He, along with a few others, had been the first to be converted to the new faith. He was then a young man who ran from the hills and went to live with the white man in the newly established Mission. He feared the revenge of the hills; the anger of his friends, betrayed. In Siriana he found a sanctuary and the white man's power and magic. He learnt to read and write. The new faith worked in him till it came to possess him wholly. He renounced his tribe's magic, power and ritual. He turned to and felt the deep presence of the one God. Had he not given the white man power over all? He learned of Jesus—

> Behold, a virgin shall conceive,
> And bear a son,
> And shall call his name Immanuel.

He realized the ignorance of his people. He felt the depth of the darkness in which they lived. He saw the muddy water through which they waded unaware of the dirt and mud. His people worshipped Murungu, Mwenenyaga, Ngai. The unerring white man had called the Gikuyu god the prince of darkness.

Isaiah, the white man's seer, had prophesied of Jesus. He had told of the coming of a messiah. Had Mugo wa Kibiro, the Gikuyu seer, ever foretold of such a saviour? No. Isaiah was great. He had told of Jesus, the saviour of the world.

> Those who refuse him are the children of darkness;
> These, sons and daughters of the evil one, will go to Hell;
> They will burn and burn for ever more, world unending.

These strong words frightened Joshua and shook his whole body; shook him to the very roots of his being. He became baptized and it was only then that he felt at peace and stopped trembling.

He felt happiness which cut sharp into him, inflaming his

soul. He had escaped Hell. He felt a new creature. That is always what he said at home and in church.

If anybody is in Christ, behold, he is a new creature.

He was washed new. He became a preacher, brave, having been freed from fear. He no longer feared Chege or what the hills and their inhabitants would say or do to him. He went back to Makuyu and preached with a vehemence and fury that frightened even his own old listeners. Few could resist that voice. Many came and some were converted. And they all together rejoiced and praised God.

But some went back to drinking; to dancing the tribal ritual; to circumcision. And Joshua day by day grew in wrath and vehemently condemned such behaviour. Perhaps the word had not taken root. Joshua himself was strict and observed the word to the letter. Religious uniformity in his own home was binding. He meant to be an example to all, a bright light that would show the way, a rock on which the weak would step on their way to Christ.

Joshua was sitting outside his house when the two girls came and put their water-barrels down. He looked at them, at the way they were working, the way they kept together, and felt a father's pride. His house had a strong Christian foundation and he wanted his daughters to wax strong in faith and the ways of God. Would this not prove to all what a Christian home should be like?

The year was unusual. The seasons were rich. Maize and beans were gathered and put aside against the uncertainties of the future. People were happy and there was much rejoicing everywhere. The group of Christians in Makuyu came together and gave prayers to God.

The elders of Kameno, and all over the country of sleeping lions, collected and gave sacrifice to Murungu under the sacred tree. All this was a prelude to many such rites which would be performed, not only by Joshua's followers in preparation for Christmas, but also by the others ready for initiation ceremonies. Joshua was against such initiation rites, especially the

30

female circumcision, which was taking on a new significance in the relationship between Makuyu and Kameno.

To Joshua, indulging in this ceremony was the unforgivable sin. Had he not been told to take up everything and leave Egypt? He would journey courageously, a Christian soldier, going on to the promised land. Nobody would deflect him from his set purpose. He wanted to enter the new Jerusalem a whole man.

In fact, Joshua believed circumcision to be so sinful that he devoted a prayer to asking God to forgive him for marrying a woman who had been circumcised.

God, you know it was not my fault. God, I could not do otherwise, and she did this while she was in Egypt.

Sometimes, when alone with Miriamu, his wife, he would look at her and sadly remark, 'I wish you had not gone through this rite.'

Not that Miriamu shared or cherished these sentiments. But she knew him. Joshua was such a staunch man of God and such a firm believer in the Old Testament, that he would never refrain from punishing a sin, even if this meant beating his wife. He did not mind as long as he was executing God's justice.

For the whole of that year things had not gone well with Joshua. People at Kameno were becoming restless and believed that it was Joshua who was responsible for the white men who these days often came to the hills. There were rumours that a Government Post would soon be built at Makuyu and that the hills would be ruled from there. In his last visit, one of the white men had announced that people in these regions would begin paying taxes to a government in Nairobi. People shrugged their shoulders, not knowing what a tax was. Nevertheless, they blamed Joshua for this interference.

Joshua did not mind this. He himself knew what a government was, having learnt about this from Livingstone. He knew it was his duty as a Christian to obey the Government, giving unto Caesar the things that are Caesar's and to God the things that are God's. That was what he wanted every Christian to do. And was the white man not his brother? Was the white man responsible for the ills of the land? No! It was the blindness of the people. People would not walk in the light. Look now at the preparations and rituals going on all over the land. Look at the sinners moving deeper and deeper into the dirty mud of sin. Moments of great anger sometimes came to Joshua. And then he would remember that he had to be patient. Prayers would soon work a miracle on the ridges. And so Joshua went on his knees. He prayed that the people should leave their ways and follow the ways of the white man.

After a prayer he would feel reassured and a calmness would settle on his face. He waited for something to happen any day but knew that he had to be patient. He sang praise. But,

O, God, look at their preparations,
O, God, why don't you descend on this wicked generation
and finish their evil ways? Circumcision is coming.
Fight by me, Oh Lord.

He felt like going out with a stick, punishing these people, forcing them on to their knees. Was this not what was done to those children of Israel who turned away from God, who would not hearken to his voice?

Bring down fire and thunder,
Bring down the flood.

Nothing happened. Preparations for initiations went on, while Joshua and his followers prepared for the birth of a saviour.

# CHAPTER EIGHT

Sunday was always a busy day for Joshua. He conducted a long service, though Kabonyi sometimes helped him. But Kabonyi was a much less compelling preacher than Joshua, who seemed to preach with a conviction arising from deep down in the heart. Prayer and singing followed, after the service was over and still more meetings in the ridges; sometimes Joshua had to make journeys into the country, from ridge to ridge.

One Sunday he conducted a particularly long service. When it was over he felt exhausted. Only the week before he had been to Siriana with Kabonyi to discuss the recent developments. Siriana was far off and they had made the journey on foot. Now he felt so worn out, especially after his sermon, that he did not wait for the usual prayers and singing outside the small Makuyu church. He found his wife Miriamu and went home with her.

Nyambura, who never waited for the singing outside, was a few yards ahead. Muthoni was not there.

They came home. She was not there either. There was nothing unusual in this: Muthoni often remained behind chatting with villagers. Nyambura, however, knew that today she had not left Muthoni behind and she was surprised when she did not find her at home.

In the evening, Muthoni did not appear. Nyambura's heart beat fast. She became restless and walked about in front of the house, trying to sing but really watching for Muthoni. When she went back inside, her heart sank when she saw the calm face of her mother. Joshua was resting in bed. Nyambura was worried at heart and dreaded the moment when Joshua would ask for Muthoni. Joshua did not allow his children out late. He was now more strict because initiation songs were going on. He would not want his children to be contaminated by them. It was perhaps lucky that he had gone to bed earlier than usual.

'I wonder where Muthoni is?' Miriamu asked, slightly puzzled. She was a peace-loving woman and she never liked unnecessary tension in the house. Her injunction to her children was always: 'Obey your father.' She did not say it harshly or with bitterness. It was an expression of faith, of belief, of a way of life. 'Your father says this—' and she expected his children to do that, without fuss, without resentment. She had learnt the value of Christian submission, and she thought every other believer had the same attitude to life. Not that she questioned life. It had given her a man and in her own way she loved and cared for him. Her faith and belief in God were coupled with her fear of Joshua. But that was religion and it was the way things were ordered. However, one could still tell by her eyes that this was a religion learnt and accepted; inside the true Gikuyu woman was sleeping.

Nyambura kept quiet. She did not know what to say. Before she could make up a suitable answer her father called out for Muthoni. He always called for Muthoni when he wanted something. Nyambura and Miriamu looked at one another as if they had just discovered Muthoni was missing. Nyambura then jumped up as if going to look for Muthoni. But she only wanted to be away from her father's fury. Muthoni had not told Nyambura that she would go. She had just slipped away from the church. Nyambura, however, had not forgotten that morning scene at the river, even though it was a number of months back.

When she came back into the house, she found Joshua standing near Miriamu, glaring hard at her.

'I tell you again. You know where your daughter is. Go! Go out and look for her.'

Night was coming. Nyambura stood at the door, cowering there. The pot on three stones was boiling over. Miriamu went out. This is what it meant to be a mother. It meant bearing on one's shoulders all the sins and misdeeds of the children. She went about, looking in all the huts where Muthoni was likely to be. She did not find her. She came back and found Nyambura had removed the pot from the fire. Joshua and Nyambura had not exchanged a word. Joshua had not bothered to ask Nyambura of her sister's whereabouts. Perhaps his anger had blinded him.

He flew at Miriamu: 'Did you find her?' Miriamu said nothing.

'Go back and find her. She cannot sleep out.'

Miriamu hesitated. Where was she to go? She felt that Joshua was being unreasonable but she did not know how to tell him, not being given to arguments. For the moment Nyambura experienced the torture of a soul torn between two loyalties with fear in front. Should she let out Muthoni's secret? What if Muthoni returned?

'But – but—' Miriamu was stammering. Nyambura could bear it no longer. She had tried her best to keep her unspoken promise to Muthoni.

'Perhaps she has gone to my aunt,' she timidly suggested. Better she had kept silent. Joshua almost jumped at her.

'What! Your aunt? To what? Tell me at once!'

Nyambura cowered under his outburst. But she showed hesitation and she kept off the moment of revelation by saying:

'I think she has gone to my aunt at Kameno.'

'To do what?'

There was no help for it. She looked at the door, ready to run out as she gathered her courage to say the one ominous word—

'Circumcision.'

'What!'

'To be circumcised.'

Before she could run out Joshua was on her. He glared at her, shaking her all the time. He was almost mad and small foams of saliva could be seen at the sides of his mouth.

'How do you know? Who told you?'

Nyambura was beside herself with terror. She thought that he would beat her. All of a sudden, Joshua released her. He let out a very small sigh. Nyambura detected in it pain and torment. She felt pity for him. Slowly he went back to the fireplace and sank down on a stool. He looked like a beast of prey experiencing defeat and humiliation for the first time. He realized that he was growing old. Then, in a measured, lifeless voice, he said:

'For once, I give you permission to go to Kameno. Go to that woman you call aunt. Tell Muthoni to come back. If she agrees we shall forget everything. If she does not, then tell her that she ceases to be my daughter.' He went back to bed.

Silence fell in the house after Joshua had announced this. Miriamu did not speak. She too had been shocked into silence by Muthoni's action which seemed to have no explanation and to stem from no motivation. She loved Muthoni and she did not want to lose her. She knew Joshua meant what he said. Tears began to run down her face. As they fell they shone, lit by the dying embers in the fire. Sometimes the fire would flicker, creating distorted shadows across the mud walls. The formless shadows moved and wavered in a mocking manner.

On the following day Nyambura brought the sad news that Muthoni had refused to return home.

Joshua sat still as he listened to this. Already he felt ashamed for being caught last night by the devil, unawares. He had now prayed, asking for strength never to be caught again in slumber. But this news was hard for him: for a man who had walked in the paths of righteousness. He remembered Job and thanked God.

From that day Muthoni ceased to exist for him, in his heart. She had brought an everlasting disgrace to him and his house, which he had meant to be an example of what a Christian home should grow into.

All right. Let her go back to Egypt. Yes. Let her go back. He, Joshua, would travel, on, on to the new Jerusalem.

# CHAPTER NINE

Harvests came and went. They had been good; people rejoiced. Such rich harvests had not been seen for years. Old men sighed with inner fear as they witnessed the hubbub of excitement, throbbing through the ridges, making things tremble. Had they not seen such happenings before in their days of youth?

The elders, then, offered many burnt sacrifices to Murungu. Who did not know what such unusual harvests portended? Who could not remember the great famine that had swept through the hills, spreading its fingers of smoke to all the land of the Gikuyu? That was before the real advent of the white men. Most of the old men had then been young. But they had never forgotten the great wealth and harvests that preceded the famine.

Chege could remember it well. He and many others thought that famine could never come any more. But it had followed in the wake of their thoughts. Chege, together with his newly-married brides and a few others, had left the hills along a secret path. His two wives did not survive the disaster. Chege was still young. He soon found himself another bride and came back to the hills. He came back to tell the people of the white man. But they would not listen. Even when the white man came to Siriana, people would not hearken to Chege's word. When Kabonyi and Joshua were converted, he broke off their former relationship. These Christians would not come to any good, he always said. He saw more than any other could see. These followers of Joshua would bring so many divisions to the land that the tribe would die.

Were these Christians not now preaching against all that which was good and beautiful in the tribe? Circumcision was the central rite in the Gikuyu way of life. Who had ever heard of a girl that was not circumcised? Who would ever pay cows and goats for such a girl? Certainly it would never be his son. Waiyaki would never betray the tribe.

In his own family, Chege had little to fear. His daughters were circumcised and all of them were well married. And Waiyaki, who had now been in Siriana for many years, was unlikely to be contaminated by the new cult. He was equipping himself to come and fight for the tribe. But sometimes Chege had qualms about his son. Would he ever fail the tribe? Would he ever fail the prophecy? At such times he experienced a sensation of defeat, of despair. Then his son would come for holidays, and Chege, though he did not say much to him, could see that all was well.

He persevered. He knew that age was now fast telling on him and that he had not many days to live and he came to pin his whole faith on the young man. It was as if his life, his heart, was being carried by Waiyaki and he feared the boy might stumble.

In this Chege did not see it as a contradiction that he, the embodiment of the true Gikuyu, should have sent his son to the very missionary centre whose existence he had always opposed. But what did it matter? He had warned the people. They had refused to take up arms. It might even be too late now to take up arms. Luckily, there were other ways of beating the white man. For the prophecy still held good. In its fulfilment lay the hope of the people. He had learnt a lesson and he taught it to his son. It is good to be wise in the affairs of the white man.

And so Chege waited and hoped. He watched Waiyaki, his progress and his behaviour. He lived in the son. If the prophecy had not been fulfilled in him, well, there was the son. What was the difference? A saviour shall come from the hills. Good. Waiyaki was the last in the line of that great seer who had prophesied of a black messiah from the hills. The boy was doing well at Siriana. He had early gone through the second birth. And this season he would be initiated into manhood. This would help him to absorb the white man's wisdom more quickly and help the tribe. And this was what he wanted; to see

Waiyaki become a man before he himself died; then he could be sure that the work he had begun – no, the work begun a long time ago by Mugo – would not perish. You could more readily trust a man than a *kihii*, an uncircumcised boy.

The sacrifices went hand in hand with preparations for the coming circumcision. Everywhere candidates for the initiation were gathering. They went from house to house, singing and dancing the ritual songs, the same that had been sung from the old times, when Demi were on the land.

Waiyaki was one of the candidates. He was now a young man with strong, straight limbs. He did not like the dances very much, mainly because he could not do them as well as his fellow candidates, who had been practising them for years. After all, it was soon after his second birth that he had gone to Siriana, and he had lived there for all those years, although he normally came home during the holidays. Waiyaki was often surprised at his father, who in some ways seemed to defy age. His voice, however, thin and tremulous, betrayed him. Waiyaki often remembered why he was sent to Siriana. But with years the dream had grown less vivid and less real. He saw it mainly as an illusion, an old man's dream. Yet he worked hard in school. He was now in the senior class in Siriana Secondary School and he was able to meet boys from all over Kenya.

Waiyaki's absence from the hills had kept him out of touch with those things that most mattered to the tribe. Besides, however much he resisted it, he could not help gathering and absorbing ideas and notions that prevented him from responding spontaneously to these dances and celebrations. But he knew that he had to go through the initiation. And he did not like to disappoint his father. For Waiyaki knew that the old man would die in that dream of the future which had probably been a real, essential part of his life. Not that Waiyaki disliked the idea of circumcision. On the contrary, he looked forward to it. It was his boy's ambition to test his courage at the ceremony. In fact, he considered Livingstone, for all his learning and holiness, a little dense in attacking a custom whose real significance

**39**

in the tribe he did not understand and probably never would understand.

Above the beating of drums and jingles, shouts rose from hill to hill to keep awake those who might want to go to sleep. Tonight was the eve of the initiation day; it would see the biggest of all dances.

Waiyaki's mind was unsettled. He could remember nothing that had so shaken him since that famous journey to the sacred grove. But that was now a dream. This thing was real, was in everybody's mouth. All the time Waiyaki kept on wondering 'Why should she do it?' And he felt a desire to speak with her, to hear it from her own mouth. Muthoni's revolt had rung from hill to hill as if the news were passed by the wind and the drums. Her name was whispered from hearth to hearth. Waiyaki had seen her the day before in a house where she had gone for a dance. But then he had not believed it, when one of the candidates had pinched him on the back and pointed to a young girl, jumping and swinging her hips from side to side in the midst of a group of dancing women.

'That is Muthoni.'

'Which Muthoni?'

'Joshua's daughter, of course.'

'Joshua's daughter! Joshua's daughter.'

The thing seemed incredible. He had known Muthoni when she was small. He could remember the day he and Kinuthia and Kamau had made Muthoni scream with terror when they had ambushed her at Honia. Waiyaki had felt pleasure which had later turned to shame. It was no bravery frightening away girls, he had thought. Later his mother had beaten him after discovering that he had taken part. Fortunately the matter was hushed up between the women and Chege and Joshua never came to know about it.

And now here she was. Waiyaki had seen Joshua a number of times, both in Makuyu and at Siriana. He had heard of his strictness in matters concerning religion, which meant all matters concerning life. How could she have come here?

Perhaps she had run away. Lots of girls had done it. At least that is what he had been told by boys who had come from 'the beyond', where missions had long been established. The same night Waiyaki had sought out Kinuthia. Kinuthia too was a candidate for initiation.

'You surprise me,' Kinuthia had laughed at him. 'Haven't you heard that she has run away?'

The idea that she had actually run away, actually rebelled against authority, somehow shocked him. He himself would not have dared to disobey Chege. At least he could not see himself doing so.

So tonight Waiyaki knew that Muthoni had actually run away. Her aunt, living in Kameno, was going to take charge of her. In some villages people could not believe this. They said that Joshua had a hand in it, probably to appease the angry gods of the outraged hills. Was it not known that Joshua took beer secretly? Strangely, nobody had ever seen him drinking. But they said they knew.

The dance was being held at an open-air place in Kameno. Whistles, horns, broken tins and anything else that was handy were taken and beaten to the rhythm of the song and dance. Everybody went into a frenzy of excitement. Old and young, women and children, all were there losing themselves in the magic motion of the dance. Men shrieked and shouted and jumped into the air as they went round in a circle. For them, this was the moment. This was the time. Women, stripped to the waist, with their thin breasts flapping on their chests, went round and round the big fire, swinging their hips and contorting their bodies in all sorts of provocative ways, but always keeping the rhythm.

They were free. Age and youth had become reconciled for this one night. And you could sing about anything and talk of the hidden parts of men and women without feeling that you had violated the otherwise strong social code that governed people's relationships, especially the relationship between young and old, man and woman.

Waiyaki still felt uneasy. Something inside him prevented him

**41**

from losing himself in this frenzy. Was it because of Muthoni? He wondered what Livingstone would say now if he found him or if he saw the chaos created by locked emotions let loose. And the words spoken! Even Waiyaki was slightly embarrassed by this talk of forbidden things. Perhaps this was so because the mention of forbidden things at any other time was a social taboo. Of course, Waiyaki knew that nothing bad would happen in spite of the talk. It was actually a taboo to go with a woman on such an occasion.

And then Muthoni appeared on the scene. The singing increased in volume and excitement. And she was a wonder. Where had she learnt this? Waiyaki wondered as he watched from the side. She danced, sang; describing love; telling of relationships between a woman and a man; scenes and words of loving-making. The missionaries in Siriana would certainly have condemned her to eternal hell. Waiyaki gazed at her. Something slightly stirred in him. In the yellow light she appeared beautiful and happy, a strange kind of elation.

Somebody pulled him into the circle. It was Kinuthia. 'Dance!' the girls shouted, pulling him along the circle and repeating some of the hip motions for him. At first that thing inside him kept him aloof, preventing him from fully joining the stream. Although his body moved and his mouth responded to the words, his soul did not fully participate. Then, from a corner, he heard his name. They were singing for him, some praising him and others making jibes at him. The name was taken up by the drummers and the soloists.

The frenzy and shrieks were up again. And suddenly he felt as if a hand soft and strong had held his soul and whipped it off. It was so strange that he felt his emotions and desires temporarily arrested in a single timeless moment; then release. Waiyaki was nothing. He was free. He forgot everything. He wanted only this thing now, this mad intoxication of ecstasy and pleasure. Quick waves of motion flashed through his flesh, through his being.

He was given a horn. He blew it madly. He jumped and swung his hips and did all sorts of marvels with his body. The others tried to follow him. Muthoni's secret was out. You did not have to learn. No. You just gave yourself to the dream in the rhythm. Within a few seconds he found himself face to face with Muthoni. Both had been thrown into the centre.

And she seemed to hold him still. Not with hands. Not with anything visible. It was something inside her. What was it? He could not divine what it was. Perhaps her laughter. He thought there was magic in it because it rang into his heart, arousing things he had never felt before. And what was shining in her eyes? Was there a streak of sadness in them? For a time Waiyaki was afraid and looked round. His mother was watching them. He turned to Muthoni. The magic was not there any more; it had gone. In the next moment Waiyaki found himself wandering alone, blindly away from the crowd, wrestling with a hollowness inside his stomach. He felt hurt. He had laid himself naked, exposed himself for all the eyes to see.

He ran into her in the darkened fringe of the trees. She stood there and the only communication between them was quiet breathing, as if each had his own devil to wrestle with.

'You are a rebel,' he said, almost unconsciously.

'Yes – I am,' Muthoni answered defiantly.

'Why did you do it, Muthoni?' he asked with bitterness.

'Do what?'

Waiyaki felt foolish. The words had just formed and he had meant to speak to her gently, coaxing the story out of her. And now he relented. He stammered with confusion.

'I – I mean – eh – eh – running – going away from your father.' She did not answer at once. There was silence between them. They could not see each other in the darkness but they felt each other's presence by their breathing. Then she spoke, in a clear voice but slightly vibrant with sadness.

'No one will understand. I say I am a Christian and my father and mother have followed the new faith. I have not run away from that. But I also want to be initiated into the ways of the tribe. How can I possibly remain as I am now? I knew that my father would not let me and so I came.' Her voice seemed to change. Yet she was speaking in the same tone. Waiyaki, however, felt as if she had forgotten him, as if she was telling her story to the darkness. 'I want to be a woman. Father and Mother are circumcised. But why are they stopping me, why do they deny me this? How could I be outside the tribe, when all the girls born with me at the same time have left me?'

Muthoni's words seemed to be opening a new world to Waiyaki. Yet he could not see it clearly. He was being carried by her voice as it vibrated.

'I want to be a woman made beautiful in the tribe; a husband for my bed; children to play around the hearth.' It was a dream in which he was being carried, forgetting himself and the place where he stood. He remembered such another dream, long ago. But this was of a different nature, stirring violent and contradictory forces in him: 'Yes – I want to be a woman made beautiful in the manner of the tribe. . . .'

And she moved away in the dream with the dream and the darkness. Waiyaki remained where he was standing, feeling slightly dizzy and numb. Gradually he woke from his numbness. He was troubled. He walked back to the crowd. But he now knew that they would not catch him again for he was apart from it all. That night a feeling that he lacked something, that he yearned for something beyond him, came in low waves of sadness that would not let him sleep.

# CHAPTER TEN

There was mist everywhere. It covered Kameno, Makuyu and the other ridges in its thin white greyness. It was chilling, chilling the skin. But Honia river flowed on as if defying the mist. The water, however, was cold.

To Waiyaki, bathing so early in the morning, the water seemed to cut his skin like a sharp knife. He shivered a little as he sat, naked, near the banks of the river. The cold water had gone through the skin, numbing the muscles. His arms, bent at the elbow, rested on the knees. The palms were folded tightly into a fist, so that the knuckles of the fingers appeared like little swellings. The thumbs passed between the first and second fingers and pointed upwards. His penis had shrunk in size and, as Waiyaki looked at it, he wondered if it really belonged to him. Waiyaki was not alone. All along the banks the other initiates sat, waiting for the 'surgeon'.

All his life Waiyaki had waited for this day, for this very opportunity to reveal his courage like a man. This had been the secret ambition of his youth. Yet, now that the time had come, he felt afraid. He did not, however, show it. He just stared into space, fear giving him courage. His eyes never moved. He was actually seeing nothing. The knife produced a thin sharp pain as it cut through the flesh. The surgeon had done his work. Blood trickled freely on to the ground, sinking into the soil. Henceforth a religious bond linked Waiyaki to the earth, as if his blood was an offering. Around him women were shouting and praising him. The son of Chege had proved himself. Such praises were lavished only on the brave.

Waiyaki sat still after the surgeon had left him. He was now covered with a white sheet. All was well. Yet the pain came and shook him to the roots. What was Muthoni feeling, he wondered. He thought that if he had been in her position he would never have brought himself into such pain. Immediately he hated himself for holding such sentiments. He was of the tribe. He had to endure its ways and be inside the secrets of the hills.

His childhood days came and fleeted by. Many things clouded his mind; his early adventure; the years at school. He thought of Livingstone. What would he now think if he found Waiyaki sitting there facing the river, holding his penis with blood dripping on to his fingers, falling to the ground, while a white calico sheet covered him? Waiyaki wanted to laugh at the monstrous idea of Livingstone standing and watching all ... a-a-a- ... the numbness was wearing away ... the skin alive again ... pain ... Waiyaki could not move. The pain was eating through him. That was the gate to the mystery of the hills. And that day when Chege took him to the sacred grove appeared vividly for a second. Then the experience lost its clear edges ... most ... strange how that old men defied time ... had Waiyaki understood him? Something always held Chege aloof from everything around him. Livingstone in his way was like Chege ... standing for the other side ... no ... confusing the two ... the pain again, biting like ants eating into the flesh ... oh ... two strong waves ... his mind was wandering. Steel yourself, Waiyaki. Keep still. ...

A shout and cry mixing with suppressed groans of pain! Women were shouting and singing their bravery. All was over. The new generation had proved itself. Without a single blemish.

The hospital was a small shed a little distance from the village. The floor was hard with bumps. A thin covering of grass and banana leaves was their bed. After two days Waiyaki's wound had swollen so much that he began to doubt if he would ever be well again. Perhaps he would lose his manhood. He shuddered. The other initiates were like him. And whenever the attendants came to treat them, a few initiates screamed with pain as soon as the swollen part was pressed. Food was plentiful but who had any taste for it? They were forced to eat with teasing threats that their 'thing' would be cut. A more serious threat was that a woman might be brought into the shed and one of the attendants would make love to her in their presence. The initiates were horrified and the attendants laughed. Everybody knew how painful the whole thing would be at the slightest provocation of that kind.

The only relief was when the attendants told them stories of men and the inner secrets. At first such stories were intolerable to Waiyaki, especially as he had to listen to them. It was part of their education. But after a few days, when his wound became better, he found that he could listen to the stories with relish and enjoyment. He had a lot to learn.

'They are all out now?'

'Yes. We are happy. The boys have been a credit to the hills.' Pride, indeed, could be detected in Chege's voice. He had a reason for this. Everywhere he went, he received compliments on the way his son had emerged from the whole experience. People were amazed that the white man's education had not softened him; he could stand the traditional ordeal without flinching.

'And the girls?' The elder from Gathanjo asked.

'All . . . all . . .'

'Yes?' the elder queried. He saw that Chege was hesitant.

'There is a girl . . . she is not well.'

'Who is she?'

'Muthoni.'

'Oh, Joshua's daughter? We heard about her. Strange case for a girl. . . .'

'It is strange,' agreed Chege. A little silence fell between them. The sun was high up in the sky and the two men had taken shelter under a tree.

'Yes . . . it is strange,' repeated Chege. 'All the other girls have left, their wounds nearly dry scars.'

'And she? Left in the . . .'

'Oh, no. She stays with her aunt. Her wound, we hear, is getting bigger and worse.'

'A father's curse.'

'Maybe.'

'These Christians. They will never come to any good,' the elder commented slowly, shaking his head.

'I have always said so. You see what discord in the family does. If Joshua had not sold his heart to these people, it would have been a simple case. Why! A black ram without blemish under the Mugumo tree – simple sacrifice. And all would have ended well.'

'Yes. But now he won't agree. So obstinate has he become, I hear, encouraged by those white people. . . .' The elder stood up and took his staff. He sneezed and pulled two leaves he was carrying. He rubbed his nose. 'Well, I will go now when it is day.'

'Go in peace. These hills from the ancient times have seen strange things.'

'Stay well. Remain in peace.'

The elder went away. Chege watched him disappear. Then he stood up and looked across the valley. Through an opening in the forest, he could see the various huts that lay scattered on the opposite ridge. One side of the roof of Joshua's house could just be seen. Chege let out a small, enigmatic sigh and then murmured, 'Not well. Not well.' He took the staff and began trudging back to his home. He was glad that Waiyaki was now a man. But still he feared for the country.

Waiyaki watched her: she was breathing hard. It was now a week since the others resumed their normal life. But Muthoni was still suffering. Waiyaki had come to see her.

'How are you now?' he forced himself to say.

'I am all right,' she replied with difficulty. Her face was much darker than it had been before initiation. She was bearing it well. Waiyaki admired her courage, a courage that never deserted her. They talked little. At one time she turned her eyes away from Waiyaki and said, 'I wish Nyambura could come to me.' It was not a complaint. It was just a wish, a longing that she hoped might be fulfilled.

'Why does she not come?'

'I think my father would not allow her.'

'It is cruel,' Waiyaki said, having nothing else to say.

'I disobeyed him. I chose my way and when he called me back, I refused to go.'

Waiyaki let his eyes roll around the darkened walls of the hut. Black soot hung from the roof in strings, as if ready to fall. Muthoni's bed was made of bamboo poles tied together to make a frame. Other sticks were tied across. The bedding was grass mixed with a few pieces of sacking and banana leaves. The bed was low, against the wall, just near the door. Waiyaki thought: 'Is she paying for the disobedience?' He shrank to think of this. Was everyone to pay with suffering for choosing his way, for being a rebel?

'And your mother—?'

'She too would not come. He would not allow her.' She paused a little. 'And I would not want her to come. She would only cry and become sad and I would rather bear the pain alone.'

When Waiyaki left the hut, his mind was made up. He must see Nyambura. And that day he went to Makuyu and strolled about; hovered around Joshua's household, hoping to meet her. There was something in Muthoni that somehow called forth all his sympathy and admiration. Was he himself capable of such a rebellion? But he reflected that it was only proper to obey one's father. Perhaps Muthoni had been wrong to disobey. His did not see Nyambura that day.

The following morning he found her drawing water from Honia river. He did not know her very well; but he was struck by the resemblance between the two girls. Even her eyes had that restless but clear look noticeable in Muthoni. Waiyaki did not waste words with her. After greetings, he told her about Muthoni and the condition in which she was. Nyambura was shocked and wept with bitterness. This was embarrassing for Waiyaki and he quickly excused himself, after warning her not to tell Muthoni that it was he who had been to call Nyambura. Nyambura did not wait but immediately left her waterpot and went to see Muthoni.

And after that first visit, she came more often. She avoided the vigilance of her father and would come and stay with Muthoni for as long as possible, chatting about a number of irrelevant things. Sometimes tears suddenly gushed from her eyes and she could not hold them back.

'Why did you do it? Why did you—?' she would ask, her love for her sister mingling with bitterness. Muthoni would try to smile and say, 'I wanted to be a woman. One day, Nyambura, you will know.'

'Let me never know, let me . . .'

'You too will have to make a choice one day.'

'Oh, Muthoni. Why did you—?' And she would not proceed.

As days went by, Muthoni became worse. Waiyaki, who was a frequent visitor, grew more troubled. Muthoni was wasting away so fast. Now only her eyes seemed to have any life. Something had to be done. He was now convinced that the herbs which the aunt gave to Muthoni would not cure her. He consulted Nyambura and she agreed with him. The two then approached the aunt and Waiyaki gathered enough courage to say:

'Muthoni should go to hospital.'

'Where?' the aunt asked rather hopefully.

'Siriana Mission hospital.'

For a few days Muthoni's aunt resisted the suggestion. Nyambura beseeched her, hatred seething in her heart. She blamed her aunt for this trouble. The aunt began to give way.

'Who will take her?' she asked Waiyaki at last. Waiyaki thought a little.

'If there is nobody to take her, I shall. I can get some helpers and I know the way. It is long but we can go.'

'Come tomorrow.'

Muthoni was in a bad state. Only the day before, she had fallen into a delirium. Laughing and crying she would say, 'I am a woman now.'

On the day Muthoni was taken to the hospital Nyambura broke the news to Miriamu. She and Muthoni had agreed to

50

keep their mother ignorant for fear of bringing misery to her. But the case had reached a crisis. Miriamu broke down weeping and cried, 'Why didn't you tell me before? Oh, Muthoni!'

# CHAPTER ELEVEN

Waiyaki emerged from the smoke-clouded hut and walked away slowly, dragging his feet and shambling over things like a drunken man. The hut belonged to Njeri, the aunt of Muthoni. She had no husband for her man had died years back after an attack of strange illness. She was now a middle-aged woman for whom life had lost much of its attraction. Having no children of her own, she readily welcomed into her house any young people and children. A little while before her life had been illuminated by Muthoni, who had turned to her for refuge.

But life was not kind to her. Muthoni was now dead. As Waiyaki walked aimlessly along the ridge, he wondered what Njeri would do. For she would no doubt be blamed for the death of Muthoni. Waiyaki could see her face, which had become all at once wrinkled when she heard the sad news. It had been unbearable; that simple act of hiding her face in her hands and standing still, without tears.

Nyambura and her mother wept without speaking, without a sigh even. Only tears flowed down continuously. They had come to await the return of Waiyaki and the ten young men who had taken Muthoni to Siriana. Waiyaki was unable to look at Nyambura or her mother. He had just told the news and then after a while stumbled out of the house. It was three days since they left Kameno.

Waiyaki did not go straight home. The sun seemed to have set early. The country was dull pale orange; everything seemed strangely quiet. The cattle, returning home, did not make much noise and there were no children prancing about. Wherever Waiyaki went, the silent face of Muthoni would come and bar the way. Then he would turn away in another direction; still she was there, everywhere. Livingstone had been at the hospital. And the white women too. Muthoni remained calm and her eyes had an intense glow that had been with her all along the difficult journey. She had not been able to walk but the young men had made a stretcher and carried her on it. She had not talked much. But at times she spoke of Nyambura.

Waiyaki knew Muthoni loved her sister. He remembered a day soon after Nyambura had begun to visit Muthoni. He had entered the hut and found the two girls arguing.

'I am still a Christian, see, a Christian in the tribe. Look. I am a woman and will grow big and healthy in the tribe.'

Even after he had entered, she rambled on. She had not known how fast she was wasting away.

She did not last many hours after they arrived in Siriana. Waiyaki could still remember her last words as they approached the hospital. 'Waiyaki,' she turned to him, 'tell Nyambura I see Jesus. And I am a woman, beautiful in the tribe. . . .'

She had died clinging to that image, to that obsession which had led her from Makuyu to Kameno. Who knew what it was? The only question which people had asked was 'Why did she do it . . . ? Why? Why?' And even for Waiyaki the question remained 'Why?'

Darkness came and found Waiyaki wandering like a lost spirit. Had he too been taken by that dream? It was her secret . . . and she had died for it. He reached his own hut, recently built for him, lit the lamp and went to bed. He could not sleep and all through the night he kept on asking why. He did not know whom he was asking.

Joshua heard of the death of Muthoni without a sign of emotion on the face. A slight tremor in the voice when he spoke was the only thing that betrayed him. He did not ask Miriamu when she died or how Miriamu had learnt of the facts. Miriamu wept even more when she saw the impassive face. To him, Muthoni had ceased to exist on the very day that she had sold herself to the devil. Muthoni had turned her head and longed for the cursed land. Lot's wife had done the same thing and she had been turned to stone, a rock of salt, to be for ever a stern warning to others. The journey to the new Jerusalem with God was not easy. It was beset with temptation. But Joshua was determined to triumph, to walk with a brisk step, his eyes on the cross. Muthoni had been an outcast. Anything cursed here on earth would also be cursed in heaven. Let that be a warning to those who rebelled against their parents and the laws of God.

Chege beheld this in silence. No longer would the voice be heard; no longer would he give the warning. He had done his work. Had he not foreseen this drama? Had he not seen the estrangement between father and daughter, son and father, because of the new faith? This was a punishment to Joshua. It was also a punishment to the hills. It was a warning to all, to stick to the ways of the ridges, to the ancient wisdom of the land, to its ritual and song.

Would Joshua listen? Would Kabonyi hearken to the voice of angry Murungu? Chege feared for them. He feared for those who had embraced strange gods. Would the ridges listen and rise up together? Makuyu and Kameno still antagonized each other. Makuyu was now the home of the Christians while Kameno remained the home of all that was beautiful in the tribe. Who would ever bring them together?

The death of Muthoni did not augur well for the future; it might bring further strife. Chege did not like the way his son had become involved in the affair. He feared for him. But he admired Waiyaki; his figure and his youth. He could not say anything to him. Already he found that he could not really understand his son. Would he be corrupted by Siriana? Again he felt his bones creak. He touched his grey hairs with a sigh and meditatively watched the dying day as he sat on his three-legged stool in front of his hut. He questioned the wisdom of having sent his son to the Mission place. Would he, Chege, be punished like Joshua? What of the prophecy? He thought of going to seek a man of his generation with whom he could talk things over.

He stood up. The cold evening wind made him shake a little. He was old, old. He sighed again, but his sigh was not due to age or to the realization that his time was gone. It was the sigh of many who that night and weeks after talked of Muthoni's death. The fact was that nobody knew for sure what the death portended.

Far away in Siriana, it was a sigh with a different meaning. The death of Muthoni for ever confirmed the barbarity of Gikuyu customs.

Livingstone, the head of the Mission, had always shown reluctance in penetrating the ridges. He had always liked the idea of training some Mission boys who could then be sent out to spread the good news. He was now an old man, bald-headed, and with a double chin. He had a large pith helmet of which he was very fond. He rarely removed it from his head, but when he did, the almost sheet-white bald head made a big contrast to the freckled face, hands and feet. Whenever he moved, his knees shook a little, while his tired voice and habit of speech was characterized by a tendency to pronounce 'r' even where some of the other men and women at the Mission would not. His knowledge of Gikuyu language was tolerably good. Twenty-five years' stay at the Mission was not such a short period.

When he came to the Mission, he was full of vigour and certainly full of great expectations. He always looked to a time when his efforts would produce fruits. But as years went on he realized that he was not making as much progress as he had expected he would. This was a disappointment to a man who had left home for a wild country, fired by a dream of heroism and the vision of many new souls won for Christ through his own efforts. His call and his mission had not met with the response he had once hoped for. True, the school and the hospital had expanded a great deal. But these people seemed only interested in education, while they paid lip service to salvation.

They were entrenched in their blind customs. Children

became ill. People believed that they were bewitched. A man died. His body was abandoned without burial. And then this circumcision – it was barbarous. Livingstone was one of those missionaries who thought themselves enlightened. They were determined to learn the customs of the natives and not repeat the mistake of the missionaries of the earlier generation who had caused tribal warfare and civil strife because they could not appreciate the importance of tribal customs.

In this spirit he had attended some of the dances on the eve of circumcision. But he was horrified beyond measure. The songs he heard and the actions he saw convinced him beyond any doubt that these people were immoral through and through. He was thoroughly nauseated and he never went to such another dance. Circumcision had to be rooted out if there was to be any hope of salvation for these people. Livingstone was a man of moderation and advocated gradual methods of eradicating the custom. In spite of pressure by some great enthusiasts, he refused to adopt rash and desperate measures. This was during his early years. But when he saw that this policy of letting things happen gradually had not had the hoped-for results, he began to preach against the custom vigorously. Even then the full war was not on. Would he eventually give way to pressure? He was growing old. New blood had joined him in Siriana.

And then Muthoni died after circumcision – after this brutal mutilation of her body. People would accuse him. He felt cheated by fate. Circumstances were laughing at his old age. But he would show them that the spirit of the Lord still burnt in him. Age did not matter. It was Christ who would be fighting the Prince of Darkness through him, yes, Christ working in him, making him young in action. Circumcision had now to be fought by all means in their hands. He could count on Joshua and Kabonyi to help him.

And then a woman came to him. He was in his office and was startled to see her. Martha was one of the staunchest critics of his policy.

'Excuse me, Reverend.'

'Yes?'

'Do you know the girl who died?'

'Muthoni? She was brought by Waiyaki and some other Mission boys.'

'You don't know her father.'

'Eh . . . no.'

'She is the daughter of – of—'

'Yes?'

'Joshua!' she said rather triumphantly. There was a twinkle in her eyes. There was a short space of total silence. And then—

'Oh!' It was a small groan. Almost pathetic. The war was now on.

# CHAPTER TWELVE

Within a few weeks the name of Muthoni was a legend. Stories grew up around her name. Some people said that she had not actually died of the wound, but that she had been poisoned by the missionaries. Indeed, one of the boys who had taken her there had seen this.

The elders from Makuyu gathered together, made a few irrelevant remarks and then looked at one another. They understood. This new faith had contaminated the hills and Murungu was angry. Listen to the roaring thunder in the sky! Look at the blinding lightning flashing across the earth! They remembered Chege and his words. They ought to have listened to him. The white man should never have set a foot in Siriana. A Government Post was being built on the ridge next to Makuyu. And it was now clear that people would have to pay taxes.

What could they do? It was now too late to take action. Chege was near to dying. A strange disease of the stomach confined him to his home. Added to this was the strength of these Christians. Led by Joshua and Kabonyi they had almost established Makuyu as their stronghold. Some elders, however, argued that it did not matter. The death of Muthoni had clearly shown that nothing but evil would come out of any association with the new faith. And Chege's son? The elders feared. Chege ought never to have allowed him to be associated with Siriana.

And Joshua's followers gathered. They talked and sang praises to God. Muthoni was an evil spirit sent to try the faithful. It was now clear to all that nothing but evil could come out of adherence to tribal customs. Joshua, their leader, was inspired. He now preached with vigour and a strange holiness danced in his eyes. He had been to Siriana and explained the situation to Livingstone. Livingstone had understood. Now

Joshua came with a new message. Circumcision was wholly evil. Thenceforth nobody would ever be a member of Christ's Church if he was so much as found connected in any way with circumcision rites. The fire in Joshua gave new strength and hope to his followers. The white men in Siriana and other places were behind them. And with them all – God.

Waiyaki did not go back to Siriana. His father was very ill and he could not leave him alone. Waiyaki watched his father with fear. He could not visualize a home without him. What would he do? What would the hills do? He cast his mind back and saw the father he had always seen, yet had not really known. What kept Chege always aloof even when he stood near you? Was it his concern for the tribe? Was that the old man's dream to which he clung day by day, every hour of his life? Waiyaki remembered that day in his childhood. That was the closest he had come to understanding his father. It was as if Chege had laid his soul bare for a second to the young boy. He had never again lain so exposed. It was strange that Waiyaki should now recall the event so vividly, especially as it had for a long time been fading in his mind, losing its clear edges.

Had the missionary come to widen the split between Makuyu and Kameno? He saw the two ridges glaring at one another menacingly. Were they going to fight it out between themselves, the missionary encouraging his followers?

What surprised Waiyaki were the unprecedented feelings of hatred roused by Muthoni's death. Yet the event by itself looked small. Perhaps it was one of those things in history which, though seemingly small, have far-reaching consequences. Girls had been initiated before. But even the one or two who had died never aroused such ill-will between the people.

Waiyaki saw greater splits coming. He knew that the strictness now adopted by Livingstone would alienate even those who had taken to the new ways. Some would not entirely abandon their customs as now advocated by Joshua.

He did not wait long for the split. It came from the most

unexpected direction. Kabonyi, the great friend of Joshua, was the first to break away. He was followed by many others. Joshua remained loyal. He gathered the remnants together and they comforted each other like the disciples of old. Waiyaki's heart sank with heaviness because of this unrest. Where was his place in all this? He felt a stranger, a stranger to his land.

One day Waiyaki was returning home from a distant hill. He had gone there to meet a friend and get a shrub which had been recommended for his father. Chege would never hear of eating the white man's medicine after what happened to Muthoni. It was while he was there that he heard the news. The children of those who defied the laws of the Church and continued with their tribal customs would have to leave Siriana. And no child of a pagan would again be allowed into school unless the child was a refugee. Even then the child would have to renounce circumcision. Waiyaki knew that to be the end of him. He had hoped he would finish his final year, for he loved learning. He came home with a downcast face. He felt unwell and wanted to go to his hut and stay there by himself.

When he came home, he found his mother standing outside. She was weeping. Waiyaki was surprised and immediately forgot his own thoughts. He had never seen his mother's tears.

'What is it, Mother?'

She burst into fresh sobs. 'What is it?' he asked again with fear. Just then he saw a group of elders come out of his father's hut. He threw the shrub away bitterly and ran towards the hut, hoping against hope that he would see him alive, even if for a second.

# CHAPTER THIRTEEN

Drip! Drip! All along the edge of the corrugated-iron roof. Drip! Drip! All in a line, large determined drops of rain fell on the ground as if they were competing. They made little holes – little basins, scoop-like. Drip! That fat one was transparent and clear. Down it fell into the small basin its sisters had patiently helped to make. It struck the pool of water in the hole and muddy water jumped up, forming an impatient cone-shaped pillar. And all along the ground the cones jumped up, up like soldiers marking time. The grass outside, which for a long time had been scorched and sickly, was now beginning to wake up refreshed. And the rain came down in a fury, the straying thin showers forming a misty cloudiness so you could hardly see a few yards away. The jumping cones were doing it faster and faster. Soon the dripping stopped and was replaced by jets of water from the roof. They carried on the race.

As Waiyaki stood at the door of his office, his left foot on the lower strut and supporting himself with his hands held firmly against the side frames, he watched the slanting raindrops meditatively. The barrack-like mud-walled building, made of poles and thatch, could vaguely be seen through the misty rain, standing as it had done for about three years now. This was all the school: his office plus the building which was divided into four classrooms. Waiyaki knew only too well what was happening inside. The rotting grass thatch was no deterrent to rain. Numerous pools of water must have already formed on the floor. This was the price the education-thirsty children had to pay. Probably they were all huddled together in groups, shivering maybe in a dry corner. The lucky ones had something to cover their heads with.

Inside the office, his fellow-teachers, Kamau and Kinuthia,

were arguing over something. Both were sitting on the podo-table as was their custom. They came there because the office was also the staffroom. Whenever they had a meeting, a talk, an argument, or sometimes a quarrel, they came here. They talked politics, religion, women, anything. On the floor at the two corners nearest the door were two heaps of miscellaneous objects. The office was also the storeroom. The school equipment was stored there. It was almost hopeless to try and keep things in proper order for any length of time.

The rain poured on. Waiyaki watched, thinking confusedly about the school and the country of the sleeping lions. The country could now no longer be called isolated. Since the alienation of all the land in the hills and ridges around Siriana to white settlers, the country of the sleeping lions was like any other part of Gikuyu country. As his father had once told him, the arm of the white man was long. The conquest of the hills was well under way. Some people were already working on the alienated lands to get money for paying taxes.

'It is bad. It is bad,' Kinuthia was saying. 'I say the white man should go, go back to wherever he came from and leave us to till our land in peace.' The rest was drowned by the falling rain. It was as if Kinuthia were commenting on the thoughts passing through Waiyaki's mind.

Kinuthia was normally calm. But when he had an argument, his slow-moving eyes would change and dance with excitement. Then he would speak, waving his arms in the air. A short man with powerfully built shoulders and a determined little chin, he had a way of forcing his point home more by the vehemence of his voice than by cool logic. The political discussions held in the office were a sign of what was happening all over the ridges. There was indeed a growing need to do something. This feeling had been strengthened by this most recent alienation of land near Siriana forcing many people to move from places they had lived in for ages, while others had to live on the same land, working for their new masters.

The break with Siriana made the situation worse and inflamed the people the more. They felt the bite of injustice.

62

Some felt the ridges had slept for too long. Chege's warnings were now recalled and people wished they had responded to the call in the very early days. Small organizations sprouted in the hills. Waiyaki always found himself involved. Already they had come to see him as a leader and they instinctively turned to him for small things. But Waiyaki was always worried by thoughts of the ever-widening gulf between Joshua's followers and the breakaway elements.

Waiyaki's heart warmed towards Kinuthia. But he could never feel the same warmth for Kamau. Kamau, the son of Kabonyi, once Joshua's follower and now the leading man among those who had broken ties with Siriana, was thin and tall. But probably he was not as tall as many people had expected when he was a boy. His eyes, however, retained the same strained look. Waiyaki never liked the way Kamau looked at him with his small, sunken eyes, their white flecked brown. They gave him that appearance of cunning that Waiyaki detested. Kamau did not like him either. A young man who rises to leadership is always a target of jealousy for his equals, for those older than himself and for those who think they could have been better leaders. Kamau was a neat man with his hair always close-cropped. But there seemed to be something uncanny, something almost inhuman in his neatness—

The rain came down with greater vigour.

The heated argument still went on and Waiyaki contemplated the rain and the country, the edges of his thoughts becoming blurred.

'Suppose your father—'

'We are not talking about my father,' Kamau interrupted. Waiyaki turned his head slightly and detected a frown on Kinuthia's face. There was a tense atmosphere in the room. Then suddenly Kinuthia laughed. He was joined by Kamau. Long ago these two had fought on the question of fathers.

'You should be patient, Kamau,' Waiyaki put in. He too was joining in the laughter. Kinuthia resumed almost at once.

'Of course I mean your father as an example – for example, you see.

'I shall take my father, for example, if you like. He is the head of the family. Suppose another man, Karanja or Njuguna for example, comes in and we offer him hospitality. Suppose after a time he deposes my father and makes himself the head of the family with a right to control our property. Do you think he has any moral right to it? Do you, Waiyaki? And do you think I am bound by any consideration to obey him? And if conditions become intolerable, it lies with me to rebel, not only against him but also against all that is harsh, unfair and unjust. Take Siriana Mission for example, the men of God came peacefully. They were given a place. Now see what has happened. They have invited their brothers to come and take all the land. Our country is invaded. This Government Post behind Makuyu is a plague in our midst. And this hut-tax . . .'

He was exhausted. He looked around defiantly and yet sorrowfully. Then he began to breathe hard. He was becoming excited again. He waved his hands in the air and then gave a thud on the table. He let his eyes roll around as if he were speaking at a big political rally. Waiyaki had never seen Kinuthia like this before. And why should they, who had been educated at Siriana, be so vehement against it? It was just like his father, who had sent him to the Mission to which he had all his life objected. Perhaps life was a contradiction. Waiyaki felt something stir in him as he listened to Kinuthia. Perhaps Kinuthia was speaking for the sleeping hills, for the whole of Gikuyu country. Then he suppressed the feeling and thought of the new drive in education. Perhaps this was the answer to a people's longings and hopes. For a moment he became lost in his contemplation of education and the plans he had in mind. . . .

'Come, Waiyaki. Tell us about this new Kiama.'

It was Kamau who asked. Waiyaki lost his vision but he still watched the rain. This rain was a blessing; and the famine which people had feared would come if the drought had continued would now be averted. From the scoops flowed little narrow streams that ran through the grass. They mingled and flowed on to join the main stream, like a small river, like

Honia. Or like a flood. Only this one would end and Honia river would for ever flow.

And the small river went down making a small murmuring sound, talking to itself, or to the ground. 'Noah's flood,' Waiyaki thought.

Kinuthia spoke.

'Yes. I think such a Kiama, to preserve the purity of our tribal customs and our way of life, should be formed now.'

Waiyaki had heard about this Kiama. He knew the drive came from Kabonyi. Waiyaki feared they would give him a place in the leadership of this Kiama, which was meant to embrace all the ridges. He did not feel enthusiastic about it. He wanted to concentrate on education. Perhaps the teaching of Livingstone, that education was of value and his boys should not concern themselves with what the government was doing or politics, had found a place in Waiyaki's heart.

It rained on, the downpour almost slashing the sun-scorched grass. What was it? And still it rained, with the little streams gathering and joining together. He saw what they were doing—

> Carrying away the soil.
> Corroding, eating away the earth.
> Stealing the land.

And that was the cry, the cry on every ridge. Perhaps the sleeping lions would sleep no more, for they were all crying, crying for the soil. The earth was important to the tribe. That was why Kinuthia and others like him feared the encroachment of the white man. They feared what had happened in Kiambu, Nyeri and Muranga. The new settlers and Siriana wore the same face. And Waiyaki was thinking, was Mugo wa Kibiro right? One day the white man would go. And for a time Waiyaki remembered his father and that prophecy.

Suddenly he became angry, not with the white man or Kinuthia. He was angry with the rain. The rain carried away the soil, not only here but everywhere. That was why land, in some parts, was becoming poor. For a time, he felt like fighting with the rain. The racing drops of water had turned to filth and mud. He subsided. He now felt like laughing heartily. Even here in this natural happening, he could see a contradiction. The rain had to touch the soil. That touch could be a blessing or a curse. Waiyaki was a man of strong emotional moods.

The rain stopped. The little streams continued carrying away the soil. Now it was time to break up; the whole afternoon had been wasted. There was no way out; it had always to be like this. He would speak with the elders and see what could be done about the roof.

'I think we had better let the children go,' Waiyaki told the others. 'Kamau, will you tell them to bring jembes and spades tomorrow? We might think of mudding the building now that it has rained and there is plenty of water.'

The building certainly needed this. Even from where he stood, he could see big gaping holes along its ragged sides.

The bell, a piece of iron hanging outside by a string, was struck. A few minutes later cries and shouts of children could be heard everywhere. School was over for the day.

# CHAPTER FOURTEEN

Marioshoni, as Waiyaki's school was called, was well known in the country. Already it had a history. It was the first people's own school to be built since the break with Siriana. It had been Waiyaki's idea and even now he could not understand fully how his idea had borne fruit so quickly. He saw it as something beyond himself, something ordained by fate. Event had followed event in quick succession, quickening the rhythm of life in the hills. There had been the harvest; then Muthoni's death; the tightening of Siriana's Mission laws to the extent of not admitting to the school those who were the children of darkness, whose parents had not renounced the whole concept of circumcision. Waiyaki could still remember the excitement and the tension created along the ridges by these events.

His father's death had almost numbed him. He could not tell why, but Chege's death, though not unexpected, came as a shock to him. It seemed unfair that Chege should have died at that particular time. He should have lived longer. And Waiyaki had gone on like a man drugged, not knowing what to think or do. He had all of a sudden become a grown man. He was now on his own. It was while he was in this mood that the idea of schools had come to him. But what could he do, he being so young? And what had happened meant that he would never go back to Siriana. His time to work and serve the people had come.

In starting self-help in education, Waiyaki had seen it as a kind of mission. It was a vision which he followed with hope and passion. He travelled from ridge to ridge, all over the country of the sleeping lions. He found a willing people. Yes, the ridges were beginning to awake. The trees, the birds and the paths he trod, all knew him, knew a man destined to serve his country.

But here was not the only place where this sort of thing was happening. This new spirit simultaneously surged all over the Gikuyu country, from Kerinyaga to Kabete.

Schools grew up like mushrooms. Often a school was nothing more than a shed hurriedly thatched with grass. And there they stood, symbols of people's thirst for the white man's secret magic and power. Few wanted to live the white man's way, but all wanted this thing, this magic. This work of building together was a tribute to the tribe's way of co-operation. It was a determination to have something of their own making, fired by their own imagination.

But it was more than this. Circumcision was an important ritual to the tribe. It kept people together, bound the tribe. It was at the core of the social structure, and a something that gave meaning to a man's life. End the custom and the spiritual basis of the tribe's cohesion and integration would be no more. The cry was up. Gikuyu Karinga. Keep the tribe pure. Tutikwenda Irigu. It was a soul's cry, a soul's wish.

The schools were soon overflowing with children, hungry for this thing. A class held many children crammed together, while their teachers, any who could be grabbed from Siriana, sat in front and the expectant little eyes looked up to them, wanting to drink in this learning. And mothers and fathers waited, expecting their children to come home full of learning and wisdom. Parents would feel proud, very proud, when a son came in the evening with a tear-washed face.

'Beaten? There, don't cry. You are a man, and *he* is a *teacher*, you know.'

'That teacher is good. He beats them hard.' And, to the teacher passing through the village—

'Hey, Teacher!'

'Yes?'

'Beat them hard. We want them to learn.'

The children caught the enthusiasm of their parents. Perhaps they saw they were the hope and the glory of the tribe. But alongside these great changes there were some people who continued as of old, unbending to one way or the other.

Waiyaki was the headmaster of Marioshoni. He went there in the morning and went back home in the evening. It was nearly always like that. He liked it. The walk gave him time to think about many of the problems connected with education. He wanted to do a lot for all, and serve faithfully. Yet the power of hate and the ever-widening rift, generated, as it were, by Muthoni's death, was enough to worry anyone.

There were the Christians led by Joshua, men of Joshua as they were sometimes called. Their home? Makuyu. Then there were the people of the tribe, who had always been against the Mission and its faith. Kameno was, as it were, their home or base. The other ridges more or less followed this pattern. And so the ancient rivalry continued, sometimes under this or that guise. It was all confusion building up and spreading under the outward calm of the ridges. Where did people like Waiyaki stand? Had he not received the white man's education? And was this not a part of the other faith, the new faith? The Kameno group was strengthened by the breakaway group led by Kabonyi. Waiyaki felt himself standing outside all this. And at times he felt isolated.

Yet, amidst this isolation, he was proud. He was proud of the small but important role he had played in awakening the hills, the sleeping lions. And inside him he felt vaguely that it would be good to reconcile all these antagonisms.

His role, however, did not satisfy him. He still felt hungry and yearned for something that would fill him whole, a thing that would take possession of the whole of himself. That something seemed beyond him, enmeshed, as he was, in the ways of the land. Waiyaki was now a tall, powerfully built man who struck people as being handsome. Even so this was not the most striking thing about him. It was his eyes. They looked delicately tragic. But they also appeared commanding and imploring. It was his eyes that spoke of that yearning, that longing for something that would fill him all in all.

Sometimes the longing drove him to hard work. Waiyaki was capable of real hard labour. For this and his courageous determination he was liked and admired by the people of the ridges. Maybe the very spirit that was in his father had entered him.

So young. This puzzled people. The young could never be expected to lead or manage something that was big.

'Perhaps it is the white man's learning!' they said.

'No! Do you not remember him as a boy?'

'Yes – always queer – and full of quiet courage.'

'It is the line he descends from. Don't you remember his father?'

'Yes. He was—'

Waiyaki was becoming the pride of the hills and the pride of Kameno. Already they had started calling him the champion of the tribe's ways and life.

# CHAPTER FIFTEEN

He could not sleep. Thin rays of the moon passed through the cracks in the wall into the hut and fell at various spots on the floor. It was no good staring blankly at the hazy darkness in which every object lost its clear edges. Waiyaki wanted to talk to someone. That was what oppressed him: the desire to share his hopes, his yearnings and longings with someone. His plans in education. The desire for assurance and release. Twice he had tried to tell his mother, to ask her something. But each time he stood in front of her and he heard her shaky voice, he found himself talking of irrelevant things. It was strange that the tremor in her voice should set doubts darting in his soul.

After all, what was the longing, what was the something for which he yearned? Did he know it himself? Yet the hopes and desires kept on haunting him. They had followed him all his life.

He did not want to think. But thoughts came and flooded his heart. Strange chapters of his life unfolded before him. His young sister who had died early was the only person with whom he had been intimate. He had loved her, if that sort of closeness could be called love. He thought he loved the hills and their people. But they did not give him that something he could get from her. Then he had been very small, many seasons before his second birth. He wondered why he remembered that time. But she was dead. And death was the end of everything, on this earth. After you were buried, you turned into a spirit. Waiyaki wondered if his sister was a spirit. A young good spirit. Was she watching him? He turned round, rather frightened. He felt guilty.

Waiyaki was superstitious. He believed the things that the people of the ridges believed. Siriana Mission had done nothing effective to change this. His father had warned him against being contaminated by the ways of the white man. Yet he sometimes wondered. Was the education he was trying to spread in the ridges not a contamination?

He wanted to sleep. From side to side he wriggled on his bed, trying to close his eyes and shut away these thoughts that would not let him alone. He thought: There is something unexplainable in the coming of the white man. He had found no resistance in the hills. Now he had penetrated into the heart of the country, spreading his influence. This influence could be disruptive. Muthoni had died on the high altar of this disruption. She had died with courage, probably still trying to resolve the conflict within herself in an attempt to reach the light. Since her death everything had gone from bad to worse, and probably conflicting calls and loyalties strove within the hearts of many. Not many were like Muthoni in courage. Waiyaki wondered where he was. Was he trying to create order and bring light in the dark?

The image of his sister, that of Muthoni and many others followed each other across his mind in quick succession; shadows that had no concrete form; shadows that came and went; sometimes merging, forming nothing. Then, for one moment, his life became one white blur. But only for a second. Then came the mist, dark with no definition. The clear edges of life had gone. He lay still, a little frightened, not knowing what to think or how to find a way out.

The mist began to fade, slowly. The edges seemed to be forming. He could now see the outline of a shape coming into being through the thinning mist. Waiyaki waited for it to melt away into nothingness but it did not. The shape remained there, fixed, and he could not drive it away. He peered at it and for a time was fascinated by it. It was the shape of a woman and he could not make out who she was.

Even this too vanished. And still he could not sleep. It was no good sitting in bed, staring into the hazy darkness.

He got out of bed and it creaked as he stood up. He put on his clothes, quietly, with a slight inner agitation, an excitement of a lover thinking of the impending meeting with his woman.

He went out of the hut; he wanted to go to Makuyu to see Kamau, or any other person; a man maybe would understand him, a man to whom he could talk.

The moon was also awake. Her glare was hard and looked brittle. The whole ridge and everything wore a brilliant white. And the little things that in the day appeared ordinary seemed now to be changed into an unearthliness that was both alluring and frightening. Waiyaki listened for voices on the ridge but he could only hear silence. As he moved across the ridge, through small bushes and trees, the silence and the moon's glare seemed to have combined into one mighty force that breathed and had life. Waiyaki wanted to feel at one with the whole creation, with the spirits of his sister and father. He hesitated. Then the oppression in him grew and the desire to talk with someone mounted. The brightness of the moon seemed now soft and tangible and he yielded to her magic. And Waiyaki thrust out his arms and wanted to hold the moon close to his breast because he was sure she was listening and he wanted her cold breath near him. Now his muscles and everything about his body seemed to vibrate with tautness.

Again he was restless and the yearning came back to him. It filled him and shook his whole being so that he felt something in him would burst. Yearning. Yearning. Was life all a yearning and no satisfaction? Was one to live, a strange hollowness pursuing one like a malignant beast that would not let one rest? Waiyaki could not know. Perhaps nobody could ever know. You had just to be. Waiyaki was made to serve the tribe, living day by day with no thoughts of self but always of others. He had now for many seasons been trying to drain himself dry, for the people. Yet this thing still pursued him.

Suddenly he thought he knew what he wanted. Freedom. He wanted to run, run hard, run anywhere. Or hover aimlessly, wandering everywhere like a spirit. Then he would have every-thing – every flower, every tree – or he could fly to the moon. This seemed possible and Waiyaki raised up his eyes to the sky. His heart bled for her. But he could not run. And he could not fly.

All this while, Waiyaki had been moving. Soon he was down at Honia river. The crickets went on with their incessant shrilling. The quiet throb of the river echoed in his heart. He felt comforted. The water looked strange under the moon. He crossed the river and began climbing up the slope, following the cattle road that would take him to Joshua's village – Makuyu. He would go and see Kamau. It was strange how his life and Kamau's and Kinuthia's seemed to be running on the same road, always affected by the same events. When young, they used to take their herds grazing together. At Siriana, they were together. It was only after Waiyaki's circumcision that they separated for a time. Kamau was initiated a few months after the breakaway. And now they were together at Mari-oshoni. For a time Waiyaki became rapt in thoughts, about Kamau, Kinuthia and their life at school.

'Oh!' He stopped short and looked up. He had almost collided with a woman. Waiyaki did not speak another word or move. Nyambura was standing in front of him and he felt awkward.

'Oh, is it you?' he said at last, just to break the silence.

'I did not know it was you,' she hastily said and glanced back over the shoulder. 'Excuse me, I was lost in my own thoughts.'

Waiyaki had not seen much of Nyambura. And whenever they met they were like strangers. Waiyaki was thinking of a day when he had seen Nyambura coming from Honia river, a huge water-calabash on her back. He had been sitting on a raised bit of ground and he had known she would pass near where he was. At this, he had felt afraid and hidden in the bush. He had watched her trudging up the hill till she had vanished. He had felt relief. That was now many seasons past. He had not thought any more about her. Not until tonight. And all at once, Waiyaki recognized the shape in his mind that had refused to melt into nothingness.

Nyambura still feared her father. She knew that if he saw her standing there he would be angry. She was often lonely. The death of Muthoni had deprived her of the only companion she had ever had. So now she went to the river alone. She went to church alone. Now and then she would strike up a friendship with one or two girls on her ridge. But not one of them could replace Muthoni. Often Nyambura wept when she remembered her and all the places where they had been together, all the secrets they had ever whispered to one another flooding her mind. Then she would feel the pain inside her; the pain wrung dry her heart and no tears would fall. And sometimes she would run to Honia and just stay there watching the flow of the water. Then she would go home feeling at peace. So the river, especially on Sundays, was her companion. She had her own place where she often went. To her father she grew cold. Although she obeyed him in everything and thought that Muthoni had been wrong to disobey a father, she could not fail to connect Joshua with her sister's death. She still thought it a sin to be circumcised. When such a thought came, she wondered if the death had not been a punishment from heaven. But somehow, she could not accuse her sister of sinning.

'Tell Nyambura I see Jesus.' She always remembered these words and she clung to them. She was grateful to Waiyaki for bringing them to her. She wondered about him. She could never understand him. He was educated at the Mission yet he was leading the elements who had broken away from Siriana. Was it not known everywhere that it was this young man who had started the schools? Marioshoni was famous everywhere. Nyambura thought Waiyaki proud. Why, whenever they met he would never stop to talk. Perhaps he feared her father. Not that she wanted anything from him; but somehow, she often longed to discuss Muthoni's death with somebody who would understand. Waiyaki was the only person who had been close to her sister, and Nyambura could never think of Muthoni without Waiyaki coming into the picture. Sometimes she wished he had been on their side. He was so young and strong and knew so much. She would have spoken to him about many things. She rarely met him and whenever they met she always waited for him to make it possible for her to talk to him. But he always passed on after a quick greeting. A queer man. Sometimes she feared him and thought that he refused to talk to her because she was the daughter of Joshua.

Again Nyambura glanced over her shoulder in the direction of her home. She wondered whether to stop or to go on. She heard Waiyaki's voice.

'I am going to see Kamau.'

'And I Johana. My father has sent me to him to tell him to come to our home tonight.'

There was a little silence. Then they both laughed. Waiyaki's heart beat faster.

'Then we can walk together,' he suggested. They moved on slowly. He was at a loss and did not know what to say. He was thinking of this girl. Muthoni had been the cause of their first meeting. Then Nyambura had been a fairly tall girl with well-formed features. Now he could see the woman in her under the bright moonlight.

'What are you going to do there?' she asked.

Waiyaki thought: What am I going to do there? It was then that it occurred to him that he did not want to see Kamau. Not now. He too thought of the people and what they would say now if they saw them walking together. Above them the moon gazed and lit the whole land. Nyambura was not circumcised. But this was not a crime. Something passed between them as two human beings, untainted with religion, social conventions or any tradition.

'Just to see Kamau and the family.'

Nyambura felt a little angry. She thought: He is going to see Kabonyi to discuss their activities.

They came to a place where their ways parted. They stopped there and stood as if held together by something outside themselves. Perhaps it was the magic of the moon that held them both rooted to the spot. Waiyaki wanted to dance the magic and ritual of the moon. His heart beat hard, beating out the darkness. And Nyambura stood there looking as if she were the embodiment of serene beauty, symbolized by the flooding moon and the peace around.

Suddenly Waiyaki felt as if the burning desires of his heart would be soothed if only he could touch her, just touch her hand or her hair. He controlled himself. A strange uneasiness began to creep through him.

'Are you still teaching?'

'Yes—'

'I have not seen your school.'

'You should come some day. And why not tomorrow in the afternoon just after school closes? I could take you round.'

That was a good time. The teachers and the children would have gone. She agreed. They parted without even shaking hands. She left him there, standing, watching her vanishing form. He moved a few paces forward and then abruptly stopped and turned back. He did not feel like seeing anybody else that night.

# CHAPTER SIXTEEN

Four o'clock. And she had not yet appeared. The school was almost deserted. Waiyaki had given the children permission to go home earlier than usual because they had been working the whole day mudding the building. The gaping holes were no longer there. The walls looked newly built and the hut was quite respectable except for the roof. However, he thought he would speak about the roof when the parents met. The gathering might be a large one, for it would be attended by people from the other ridges. Marioshoni had established itself as the centre of the new spirit sweeping through the ridges. And Waiyaki, though young, was considered the unofficial leader of the education movement that would inevitably awaken the ridges. The day for the meeting had already been fixed.

Waiyaki waited. He became restless. Perhaps she would not come. He felt hurt and did not know what to do. All the day long, he had thought of nothing but their meeting. Whenever he heard footfalls, he had thought that it was she. And whenever he saw a head appearing, his heart beat with expectancy. His soul and senses were taut and tense.

She did not come. And he could not wait any more. He was angry and felt disappointed. For the first time he thought that she might be the conceited girl Kamau had painted her in their talks. He had then not believed it but now he knew it was true. What a proud woman! Was it because her father Joshua – or could it be—? Why had he not thought of it? She might have feared her father would discover her. For a time, he strongly felt the gap between them. It was as big as the one dividing Kameno and Makuyu.

He went home.

His mother's hut and two barns stood there defiantly; exactly as they had stood for years. His father's *thingira* had been burnt, as was the custom, after his death. Waiyaki could never think of his home without the old man coming into the picture. His father usually sat outside, until the cows were milked, the birds flew away and the sun sank home. Sometimes he would sit there under the family tree till darkness had covered the land.

Around the huts was bush, extending until it merged with the low-lying forest. The forest went down the slope to the Honia river. Beyond and across the valley facing Kameno was Makuyu, with many huts lying along the top in little clusters, indicating various households. From afar you might have thought the huts in Waiyaki's home were a part of the bush and the forest. Actually the whole place was not all bush. Small shambas were hidden from view by the trees. Now that the rain had fallen, Waiyaki knew that green life would soon appear; and peas, beans and maize would soon be flourishing, scorning the drought that had been threatening the country.

Njahi was the season of the long rains. It was the favourite season with all the people. For then, everyone would be sure of a good harvest. The peas and beans, bursting into life, gave colour and youth to the land. On sunny days the green leaves and the virgin gaiety of the flowers made your heart swell with expectation. At such times women would be seen in their shambas cultivating; no, not cultivating, but talking in a secret language with the crops and the soil. Women sang gay songs. The children too. And the plants and all the trees around, swaying a little as if they were surrendering themselves to the touch of the wind, seemed to understand the joy of mothers. You could tell by the bright faces of the women that they were happy.

Not only the women but cows and goats caught the life. They jumped about, kicking in the air with their tails twisted into different shapes. The children were also happy and the ones who were grown up looked after the very young ones. You would see them running about, wandering aimlessly as if the madness or the intoxication of the bees had caught them. So they ran and played. But they were careful not to harm the flowers. Waiyaki could still remember how he used to follow his mother to the shamba and keep on climbing up a *mwariki* tree. Occasionally a delicate squeal of a neglected baby would be heard rising above the peace of the fields. And the voice of the mother, distant, yet ringing with life and deep concern, would rise, admonishing the bigger children to take care of the young.

In the evening all went home; husband and boys bringing in the cattle and goats; women bringing home the day's gathering of what would be eaten at night. They would then sit and wait to see what the woman of the house had for the evening meal. The boys usually talked. But the man of the house would sit under the family tree, if it was not yet dark, and meditate or hold a discussion with one or two elders who might call at that time.

In the past few years things were changing; the pattern of seasons was broken. It no longer rained regularly. The sun seemed to shine for months and the grass dried. And when it fell, the rainwater carried away the soil. The soil no longer answered the call and prayers of the people. Perhaps it had to do with the white men and the blaspheming men of Makuyu.

Waiyaki lingered outside for a few minutes. He remembered his father and wondered how old he would look if he were still alive. Waiyaki had never understood him. Waiyaki often found himself trying to puzzle out the meaning of the old prophecy. Did Chege really think Waiyaki would be that saviour? Was he to drive out the white man? Was that the salvation? And what would a saviour do with the band of men who, along with Joshua, stuck so rigidly to the new faith?

Yes, Waiyaki wished he had understood better.

And always Waiyaki thought about Kabonyi. He did not know what to make of him. He had been a strong member of Joshua's followers. Yet when the time came he was the one who led those who had broken away. After the death of Chege he came to take up the official leadership of the hills. Maybe he was the destined saviour. Did Kabonyi see himself as such?

Chege had told Waiyaki that Kabonyi was probably the only other man who knew the real particulars concerning the prophecy.

Kabonyi was a member of the school's governing committee and made sure that he opposed Waiyaki's suggestions on every possible occasion. One time, when Waiyaki proposed that lavatories should be built, Kabonyi opposed it saying that the bush was as good a place. But after one or two elders had spoken the proposal was carried. Kabonyi kept silent for the rest of the meeting.

More annoying to Waiyaki, however, was Kabonyi's constant reference to his youth.

'Young man, we are old. We have seen a lot and gone through many experiences,' he would say whenever he wanted to be destructive. The other elders called him the Teacher as a sign of respect.

When darkness came, Waiyaki went inside his hut. 'Nyambura has done me wrong.' That was what he was thinking. But when he remembered Joshua and the way he had disowned Muthoni, he forgave her. After all, was he himself free from fear?

In his heart, Waiyaki knew that he would not have liked to be seen by Kabonyi standing with Joshua's daughter. He resented this and wondered if he too was becoming a slave to the tribe. His activities were being watched by everyone. His freedom was being curbed. Yet was this not what he wanted? Service! Service! Always standing by the tribe like his father and the ancestors before him. And fate was driving him to the helm of things. Very well. If they wanted him to stand by the tribe, he would do it. His father must have foreseen all this.

And Waiyaki felt proud of him. He felt proud of this man who had stood alone, singlehanded, and carried the heavy burden of the people's feelings and thoughts in his voice, although they did not heed him. And Waiyaki remembered his father with a new glow and admiration. He no longer felt bound. He would serve the tribe, serve, serve. . . .

There was nothing much in his hut: a rough bed, a table and one chair. The hut was cold and everything in it spoke of desolation. Waiyaki felt like an intruder penetrating the dark mystery of the place as he groped for the lantern. He shivered a little. But the glow in his heart warmed him.

The elders did not pay him much. He did not mind. This was a part of the sacrifice. Later they would feel grateful. That would be enough payment for Waiyaki. And he would go on with what he had begun: schools and more schools; get the white man's education, as his father had told him. But Waiyaki would not be satisfied with just more schools. Later he would want a college, the sort of institution that Reverend Livingstone used to talk so much about. Why, he might even get more teachers from Nairobi. Nairobi was far, far away. He had never been there. Still – all those plans were for the future. At present he would try to make his school grow and be an example to the others.

He watched the little flame, fluttering, setting hazy shadows on the round wall. The flame was dark on the fringes. The smoke went up, up, up— He watched fixedly, like a man gazing at a small object in a dream. Slowly he put out his little finger and tried to touch the flame. He removed it quickly. It was not good to play with fire. He felt angry, very angry for no particular reason. There was a knock at the door.

'Come in.'

The door opened.

'Hey – Kinuthia.'

'Waiyaki.'

'Is it well with you?'

'It is well.'

Kinuthia stood there for a moment. Then he went across and sat on the bed. Waiyaki looked at him. Kinuthia would not meet his eyes.

'You are coming from—'

'Home.'

'How is the ridge? I hope all is at peace.'

'Oh yes. All is well. And how is your mother?'

'I have not yet gone to see her. Shall we go to her hut and see what she has for us?'

They went to the hut of Waiyaki's mother; Waiyaki was not surprised at Kinuthia's visit. They often visited each other without warning.

'I have heard that you are in this Kiama?'

'I have no idea. Who told you?' This was true. Nobody had told Waiyaki about it.

'Well, I heard it with Kabonyi after school. Seems the elders want to make you the clerk. But Kabonyi is angry. I found him saying to everybody that you are too young to be let into the secrets of the tribe.' Kinuthia stopped. Then, in a more serious and slightly warning tone, he continued, 'I think Kabonyi does not like you. I would be careful of him if I were you.'

Waiyaki felt like laughing. But he checked himself and wondered why Kabonyi should be so against him. He had never done anything wrong to him.

His mother had finished cooking. The whole place had a gloomy atmosphere. Kinuthia remarked about this as they ate their food. Waiyaki glanced at his mother, who sat away from the fire.

He loved her. After all, he was her only son. He felt guilty that he did not spend much time with her. It was not like when he was young. Then he used to sit with her round the fire far into the night. She told him stories.

Quietly they ate their meal and then went back to Waiyaki's hut. He said:

'I think you are wrong, Kinuthia. Why should he dislike me? I have not done anything wrong to him.'

'Jealousy.'

They were silent, for a long time. Then they talked of many little things, about the villages and the school. Just before he left, Kinuthia suddenly said to Waiyaki, 'Kamau told me that he thought he saw you in Makuyu late last night.'

Waiyaki did not answer.

# CHAPTER SEVENTEEN

Whenever Joshua preached there was something fascinating in his voice. It carried a deep sense of conviction, a passionate commitment to the moral truths revealed to him through the Bible. His church was always packed full. He was the undisputed spiritual leader of God's children, all those who followed the new faith. Today he thundered: 'There is none righteous, no, not one.' There was the same sharp ringing voice commanding attention from everyone. It had lost none of its magic.

What one admired in Joshua was his fidelity. Ever since he took to the new faith he had remained true to Livingstone and his God. His own puritanism and strictness had never varied or wavered. If Muthoni's rebellion and death put him off, he did not show it. He had, in any case, disowned her. To him she never existed. What had a man of God to do with the children of the evil one?

In fact Joshua had emerged from this trial much strengthened in faith. He now preached with even greater vigour. As the spiritual head of the hills, he enforced the Church's morality with energy. All the tribe's customs were bad. That was final. There could never be a compromise. And so Joshua remained constant, preaching the word, singing the pilgrims' songs. He was certainly the most constant of all, for even Chege, who had died opposed to the new faith, had at least given in in one sense by allowing his son Waiyaki to go to Siriana.

Listening to the sermon, Waiyaki thought of Kabonyi and the new Kiama. And Joshua went on speaking, now raising his voice, now lowering it to make a point. 'For all have sinned and come short of the glory of God.'

Yes. The voice was clear, almost too clear for a man of his

age. The blazing sun shone with great intensity and the old rusty sheets that roofed the small Makuyu church could be heard making tiny cracking sounds. The whole congregation was tense and silent. They wanted to hear every single word that came from this man of God, their shepherd, a man who had proved himself a rock, invincible to the wiles of the devil.

Sitting at the back, Waiyaki could clearly see Joshua. Waiyaki did not know why he was there. It was really a surprise even to himself.

'Hath a nation changed their gods which yet were no gods? But my people have changed their glory for that which doth not profit. ... And coming to the New Testament, the Testament that you hold in your hands today, we read, "And Jesus said, Seek ye first the Kingdom of God...."'

Waiyaki was thinking: 'This man knows the Bible. He always mixes his own words with quotations from this Book of God.'

'Therefore, brothers and sisters, I tell you today, come to Jesus. Stand by Him. You see Him being taken to the Cross. Are you going to desert Him? Are you going to deny Him like Peter? Remember life here on earth is one of trials, and of hardship. Satan will come to you at night, in your own house, in your field, or even in church here, and he will whisper to you, calling you back to the old ways. "Njoroge and Joshua," he will say, "follow me. This broad and easy road you see here, this, my son, is the right way." Remember, do not hearken to that voice. Let us march with one heart to the New Jerusalem. In the fourteenth chapter of the book of St John, Jesus says: "Let not your heart be troubled: Ye believe in God, believe also in me. In my Father's house are many mansions: if it were not so, I would have told you. I go to prepare a place for you."

'That place is now ready for you and me, for the faithful, the happy band of pilgrims who will remain on the path, braving all the hardships. ... And today, O brother, if you hear his voice, harden not your hearts....'

Joshua looked around. For a moment he seemed to fix his glance on Waiyaki. But no. He was taking in all the people at once, with one sweep of his eyes. He talked of those who had found the light yet now walked not in the light. He spoke of those who wanted to walk their feet on two roads at the same time. How could you mix the two ways?

'My brothers and sisters, there is no compromise. Our Lord did not compromise when he hung on the Cross. He did not mix two ways but stood by the Light. . . .'

Waiyaki felt uneasy. He remembered that he had always wondered what to make of people like Kabonyi, where to place them. Then he moved on to himself. Where did he stand? Perhaps there was no half-way house between Makuyu and Kameno. And what of uniting the two ridges? Just now he did not know his ground. He did not know himself, and he felt Joshua's words touching a chord in the dark corner of his soul so that he was afraid. . . . And Joshua was speaking of conversion: new man, new creature, new life. He raised his voice. He condemned, he deplored. He coaxed and warned. Again Waiyaki felt guilty. Guilty of what? Perhaps of something to do with the light or something to do with being unfaithful to his father's voice of long ago – 'be true to the tribe and the ancient rites'. Yet here he was in Joshua's church. Joshua finished. For a time there was complete silence in the holy building. Then with one accord the congregation burst into a hymn, almost spontaneously:

Uhoro Mwega niuyu
Niukiite Guku gwiitu
Uhoro Mwega niuyu
Wa Muhonokia witu.

Good news is this
Which has come to this our place
It is the good news
Of Christ our Saviour.

Waiyaki stole out. He was glad to get away while they were

singing. He had felt like an intruder or a spy. And he came out of the church disturbed at heart. As the hymn reached his ears, he again felt that insatiable longing for something beyond him, something that would contain the whole of himself. Why had he come? True, he had been on his way to another ridge and had not originally planned to enter; but the fact remained that he had been inside. He tried to convince himself that the impulse to enter had nothing to do with Nyambura. But why had he been disappointed when he did not see her in the building?

Waiyaki was now in the new Kiama. An elder had been sent to tell him so. The Kiama had not yet begun working and so he did not know much about it. But it was concerned with the purity of the tribe and the ridges. If the elders saw him in church they would think that he was betraying them. Yet Waiyaki thought that he would never forsake them. He would serve them to the end. With the little knowledge that he had he would uplift the tribe, yes, give it the white man's learning and his tools, so that in the end the tribe would be strong enough, wise enough, to chase away the settlers and the missionaries. And Waiyaki saw a tribe great with many educated sons and daughters, all living together, tilling the land of their ancestors in perpetual serenity, pursuing their rituals and beautiful customs and all of them acknowledging their debt to him. He felt grateful at the thought. Perhaps this was the mission, the mission that the Sent One would carry out. Yes – Waiyaki would strive, strive. He was elated by his thoughts as he beheld this vision of greatness. Waiyaki walked with a brisk step, following the vision.

'Waiyaki!'

He turned round. His vision was gone.

'Kamau! Is it well with you?' They shook hands.

'It is well. Where are you coming from?'

'Well, eh— I was just passing on my way to the next ridge when I thought I might peep in and see what the old man of Makuyu does on Sundays.'

'Joshua?'

'Yes.'

They both stood under a tree near the road. Waiyaki looked at Kamau. Just then Nyambura passed them at a distance. Waiyaki's heart jumped. He watched her walking easily, going towards the next valley. She disappeared. He turned his eyes to Kamau, who was looking in the direction Nyambura had taken. Somehow Waiyaki became irritated. He remembered what Kinuthia had told him, and he wondered if Kamau had seen him with Nyambura.

'I am going,' Waiyaki said. Kamau did not answer. He seemed to be contemplating something. He said at last, 'What do you think of her?'

'Who?'

'That girl.'

'Which?'

'Why, Nyambura. Didn't you see her?'

'Well, no I didn't.'

Waiyaki cursed himself for telling a lie. But just then he felt himself in a wicked, malicious mood. Kamau did not take any notice of this. He was still looking in the direction the girl had taken. His thoughts soon materialized into 'I think she is a beautiful woman.' Suddenly Waiyaki became jealous, jealous for Nyambura.

She was waiting for him at the next valley. Her heart beat as she saw him approach. She did not know what she would tell him. For she felt guilty at her failure to go to Marioshoni on the day she had promised to see him. She had wanted to go but it would have been a big risk. Her father had been at home at the time. Waiyaki had never been out of her mind since that day they met in the moonlight. She was always excited at the thought of him. And her eyes shone so that sometimes Miriamu asked her what she was dreaming about. She did not know what was happening to her but she knew that since that accidental meeting she had not been the same again. And now she felt a strange longing for something that not even the river could give her.

For the last two weeks she had wanted to meet him, if only to greet him and pass. She had not been able to see him and she feared going to his school. Today she had not gone to church and she was strolling aimlessly when she saw him walking towards the valley. But when she saw him stand with Kamau she passed at a safe distance.

And Waiyaki was pleased to see her. He had not set eyes on her since that night. And there she now stood, quiet and rather reserved. She did not appear as she had in the moonlight. But he could see that she was beautiful. He approached her hesitantly, his heart beating. She smiled. He thought it a beautiful smile.

'Are you well?'

'I am well. And you?'

'I am well too.'

There was silence between them. They did not look directly at one another.

'I waited for you.'

'I am sorry I could not come.' She hesitated a little. 'I had much work at home and I – I could not get time.'

Waiyaki understood, or rather, he thought he did. He did not press the point further.

'It is all right. You can come another day.'

'Well – I don't know – maybe. If I get a chance.'

He stole a glance at her and saw how she turned her head away. And immediately he knew that she had come to meet him. And he at once wanted to tell her that he loved her. He could not do it. But he yearned for her and, as he went away, he felt a desire to hold her close to him and whisper many things to her.

Nyambura scarcely saw anything as she sped home. She began cooking because she knew her father and mother would be home soon. She just cooked like a woman in a dream. Waiyaki had told her nothing. Yet she felt a glow inside.

When her mother came back from church she saw the girl was excited.

'What is it, Nyambura? Has your stomach stopped aching?'

Nyambura remembered that it was the ache in her stomach that had prevented her from going to church. She immediately answered 'No.'

She knew this was not true.

When evening came and her father had come home, she went to bed, saying that she was not feeling well.

# CHAPTER EIGHTEEN

Waiyaki led a busy life. With teaching and organizing the schools, and now as a clerk of the new Kiama with its meetings and ceremonies, he seemed to live hour to hour in action. He was now known all over the ridges. Children knew him and hailed him as 'Our Teacher'. Old men and women also called him the Teacher. He was a man who, impregnated with the magic of the white man, would infuse the tribe with wisdom and strength, giving it new life. Waiyaki himself was much more interested in teaching and handling the children than in the organization and management of the Kiama. Yet sometimes moments of patriotism and high ideals would come to him. And then he would feel elated and would be ready to do anything for the people.

The day for the gathering of parents from all over the ridges was approaching. Waiyaki wanted to press for more schools, although he did not know where he would get teachers. He thought he might be able to persuade some to come from Siriana, otherwise he himself would go to Nairobi and try to get some. Another thing was coming into his mind. Every day he was becoming convinced of the need for unity between Kameno and Makuyu. The ancient rivalry would cripple his efforts in education. He also wanted a reconciliation between Joshua's followers and the others. The gulf between them was widening and Waiyaki wanted to be the instrument of their coming together. A word from him in the coming meeting might be a big start. Now was the time to show his stand. This was not a plan but a conviction. It had come like a temptation, at first a faint echo, then becoming a distant possibility and now a need. Would this not be a risk to his growing popularity? Yet he would try. And he was rather pleased to think that Nyambura might hear of it and think well of him.

The whole grass compound was full of women and men from every corner of the country. Some came to hear the report on the progress of their children. Others came to see the famous Marioshoni school. But others came to see the Teacher. They had heard of this young man, but had never seen him. This was a chance not to be missed. 'The Teacher' they whispered from hill to hill and the name came to signify only one man – Waiyaki. So his fame grew from ridge up to ridge and spread like fire in dry bush. Everyone saw him as the reincarnation of that former dignity and purity – now lost.

The school was neat. And the people saw everything in it, the outcome of their own efforts, the symbol of their defiance of foreign ways.

They went round the school admiring the well-mudded building. Here and there on the compound were little flower gardens whose general immaculate look was the talk of all. The parents saw this as the fruits of their labour, their sweat and patience. Their children could speak a foreign language, could actually read and write. And this had been done in spite of Siriana's stern action in refusing to admit the children of those who would not abandon the ancient rites.

Waiyaki, along with his colleagues, was most attentive. He mixed with the people and took them to various places, outlining his plans, obviously campaigning for his schemes before the real test came. People admired him. They liked the way he so freely mingled and the way he talked. He had a word for everyone and a smile for all. He pleased many. But not everybody. At such moments jealousy and ill-will are bound to work.

Kabonyi did not like it. He himself had laboured for the tribe. He had led the breakaway movement and was responsible for the starting of the people's own schools. And was he not a leader in every field? Kabonyi saw Waiyaki as an upstart, a good-for-nothing fellow, a boy with rather silly ideas. He was a mere boy in the face of someone like Kabonyi, whose age and experience entitled him to greater attention. As it was, the state of things was unnatural. Perhaps Kabonyi would not have been so hostile had the young man's place been taken by Kamau, his own son. Kamau was as good a teacher as anyone else and he was certainly older than Waiyaki. He would therefore have been in a better position to lead. Nobody could guess the extent to which Kabonyi resented the rise of Waiyaki. Alone among the people Kabonyi knew of the prophecy. He feared Waiyaki might be the sent one. And he hated this.

The meeting was scheduled to begin early. But old men always took their time. So the meeting actually started in the afternoon. Waiyaki opened the proceedings amid great silence. Though his voice was calm, his heart beat inside him. He feared the number of eyes in front of him. After the first few words he announced that the children would sing some songs of welcome. Waiyaki had not made up the songs. He had first been taught them in Siriana by a boy from the country beyond. But to the parents and the teachers who gathered there that day they were something new, something that strangely stirred their hearts and said what they felt.

> Father, mother
> Provide me with pen and slate
> I want to learn.
> Land is gone
> Cattle and sheep are not there
> Not there any more
> What's left?
> Learning, learning.
>
> Father, if you had many cattle and sheep
> I would ask for a spear and shield,
> But now—
> I do not want a spear
> I do not want a shield
> I want the shield and spear of learning.

These simple words made some shed tears. Fathers resolved to work. They would strain themselves. The white man was slowly encroaching on people's land. He had corrupted the ways of the tribe. Things would now change. It may take years, but far, far into the unknown future things would become different. A saviour had come. He had opened the eyes of the people. He had awakened the sleeping lions. They would now roar, roar to victory. The children were getting learning. And still their voices rose higher and higher.

> Father,
> The war of shields and spears
> Is now ended
> What is left?
> The battle of wits,
> The battle of the mind.
> I, we, all want to learn.

Old men and women strained their ears to catch the sweet words, their hands pressed hard on their hearts or their chins. Kabonyi was writhing within. His heart and soul burnt with anger. The 'boy' was making a favourable impression while he meant to denounce him. The 'boy' had been seen in the church of Joshua and had been seen standing with Joshua's daughter. Kabonyi had meant to shame the boy before the crowd.

But the children sang on, voicing the cry of many, speaking aloud the silent cry of generations everywhere, generations that feel their end is near unless there are changes. Were they mourning for a dead glory? Were they sorrowing over a tribe's destruction or were they hailing the changes that had yet to come? Sorrow or yearning was in their eyes. And they could see this reflected in the glittering eyes of the saviour.

The children finished singing and sat. Everywhere strange silence reigned. Then from every corner the cry was taken up and all sang with one accord—

> Gikuyu naa Mumbi
> Gikuyu naa Mumbi
> Left a land virgin and fertile
> O, come all—

When Waiyaki began to speak again he felt happy. This was the moment to push his plans through. He spoke quietly, clearly, the elation of speaking to a large crowd making him feel light. He briefly outlined his plans for Marioshoni. The rotting roof needed more tin; the children needed desks, pencils, paper. And then many more schools had to be built. More teachers had to be employed. He sat down, fearing that he had not made his point clear. But the applause that greeted him left him with no doubt about the reception of the short speech.

A moment too soon Kabonyi was on his feet. He did not smile but looked defiantly around him. The battle was on. He was old but his voice was good and steady. Besides, he knew his audience well and knew what to appeal to. He could speak in proverbs and riddles, and nothing could appeal more to the elders, who still appreciated a subtle proverb and witty riddles. Kabonyi again knew his limits. He did not want to bring too many issues together. So he decided to leave the Joshua affair and come to it later as a final blow.

He reminded them of the poverty of the land. The dry months had left the people with nothing to eat. And the expected harvest would not yield much. He touched on the land taken by the white man. He talked of the new taxes being imposed on the people by the Government Post now in their midst And instead of Waiyaki leading people against these more immediate ills, he was talking of more buildings. Were people going to be burdened with more buildings? With more teachers? And was the white man's education really necessary? Surely there was another way out. It was better to drive away the white man from the hills altogether. Were the people afraid? Were there no warriors left in the tribe? He, Kabonyi, would lead them. That was why he had formed the new Kiama. He would rid the country of the influence of the white man. He would restore the purity of the tribe and its wisdom.

'Or do you think the education of our tribe, the education and wisdom which you all received, is in any way below that of the white man?'

He challenged the people present, appealing to their pride, to the manhood in them and to their loyalty to the soil.

'Do not be led by a youth. Did the tail ever lead the head, the child the father or the cubs the lion?'

A few people applauded. And then there was silence. (Kabonyi too had stirred something in their hearts.) Soon they began to talk. Some saw a lot of truth in what Kabonyi had said. They knew they were not cowards. And surely it was easier to drive away the white man and return to the old ways! But others, especially the young people, were on Waiyaki's side. Waiyaki himself was hurt. Kabonyi had touched on a sore spot, the question of youth. When Waiyaki stood up again the old defiance came back. The courage that had made him famous among the boys of his *riika* was now with him. At first he just looked at the people and held them with his eyes. Then he opened his mouth and began to speak. And his voice was like the voice of his father – no – it was like the voice of the great Gikuyus of old. Here again was the saviour, the one whose words touched the souls of the people. People listened and their hearts moved with the vibration of his voice. And he, like a shepherd speaking to his flock, avoided any words that might be insulting. In any case, how could he repudiate Kabonyi's argument? Waiyaki told them that he was their son. They *all* were his parents. He did not want to lead. The elders were there to guide and lead the youth. And youth had to listen. It had to be led in the paths of wisdom. He, Waiyaki, would listen. All he wanted was to serve the ridges, to serve the hills. They could not stand aloof. They could never now remain isolated. Unless the people heeded his words and plans, the ridges would lose their former dignity and would be left a distance behind by the country beyond. . . .

So he spoke on, pointing out the importance of learning, of acquiring all the wisdom that one could get. People wanted him to go on, on, on telling them the sweet words of wisdom. When he sat down the people stood and, as if of one voice, shouted, 'The Teacher! The Teacher! We want the Teacher!' And some shouted: 'Our children must learn. Show us the way. We will follow.'

What more could Waiyaki want? He felt elated with gratitude and happiness.

Thereafter every elder and teacher who spoke added nothing but praise for the Teacher. An inter-ridge committee was elected to look after the education of all and see to the building of new schools in the country. Kabonyi was not on it.

'Kamau, my son!'

'Yes, Father.'

'My legs, they shake.'

'Why? Are you ill, Father?'

'Yes – no – yet my legs. They grow weak. Take my staff and lead me home.'

And those who were around saw Kabonyi being led home by his son, one of Waiyaki's teachers. And soon, with a smile, everybody knew that Kabonyi was ill. Actually he was not ill, but he was full of fury. To suffer a public defeat! A public humiliation! No. It could not be. It must not be!

'I could kill him.'

'Kill who, Father?'

They were now standing on the hill. Kabonyi looked at his son.

'You are a worthless man,' he burst out. 'Are you my son? Couldn't you have supplanted him a long time ago? What has he that you have not?'

Kamau did not answer. He too had bitter thoughts. Would he and his father always suffer under the hands of Waiyaki?

Within a few months the face of the school changed. More schools were put up on a number of other ridges. Waiyaki's fame spread. The elders trusted him. They talked about him in their homes and in the fields. Even Kabonyi seemed resigned to this young man's leadership. It was faith, unknown, unquestioning, almost smothering if one was aware of it. But he was their leader and they knew that he would never let them down.

He was a match for the white men, these men who had wanted to annihilate Gikuyu and Mumbi. The tribe would now conquer, triumphing over the missionaries, the traders, the Government and all those who had come to imitate the strangers.

If Waiyaki had been fully aware of this faith in him, he might have feared. But he was not. The idea of education had now come to him like a demon, urging him to go on, do more. Even when later he was forced by the Kiama in their extravagant enthusiasm to take an oath of allegiance to the Purity and Togetherness of the tribe, he did not stop to analyse if any danger lurked in such a commitment. Kabonyi did not exist. He saw only schools, schools everywhere and the thirst that burned the throats of so many children who looked up to him for the quenching water.

And he wanted to feel all would get this water. He even wanted Joshua and his followers to come and join hands with him. Education was life. Let it come. And with a fleeting feeling of guilt he remembered that he had forgotten to preach reconciliation.

# CHAPTER NINETEEN

All his life Joshua had tried to win more and more people to Christ. He was a man who, even at his age, had tremendous energy. And he had thought that he was succeeding. Indeed, at first he had succeeded. Many had come to him. Many had been baptized. And had he not been responsible for persuading elders to take their sons to Siriana to hear Christ's word and get the white man's learning?

But now fate seemed to be working against him. Many of those who had enthusiastically gone to him had slipped back to their old customs and rituals. Many had gone back to take a second bride. Not that Joshua saw anything intrinsically wrong in having a second bride. In fact he had always been puzzled by the fact that men of the Old Testament who used to walk with God and angels had more than one wife. But the man at the Mission had said this was a sin. And so a sin it had to be. Joshua was not prepared to question what he knew to be God-inspired assertions of the white man. After all, the white man had brought Christ into the country.

What worried Joshua was not just that many people had returned to the cursed things of the tribe like circumcision. He had even been able to come out triumphant over Muthoni's rebellion. The rise of Waiyaki as a young, intelligent leader of the tribe was the menace. Now that many schools had been built through the efforts of Waiyaki, more of his sheep might go to join Waiyaki's flock out of sheer necessity. Fearing this, Joshua got the men at the Mission to let him and the other faithful ones build a school or two where children could learn before they went to Siriana. The two schools, one in Makuyu and the other one near Ngenia, were making good progress. In time they would form a stronge challenge to Waiyaki.

The large gathering at Kameno had surprised many. It had

made Joshua realize more than he had ever done before that the forces of Satan were strong. Since that meeting, entry into Kameno, the stronghold of the devil, seemed vital. A soldier of Christ had nothing to fear. So a meeting of Joshua's followers and anybody else who wanted was arranged in Kameno.

The rally was held on a Sunday. Many Christians from the neighbouring hills attended. Some came from very far, for news of the meeting had been well spread. They sang, praised and prayed. Joshua preached with so much vigour and energy that many later said that he had been speaking with the tongues of angels. Others said that the Angel of the Lord had appeared unto him, while still others thought it was Mary who had spoken to him.

A few people were converted. That was a good beginning. For the first time in Kameno, there was a group of Joshua's men. No doubt more would follow. This was a challenge to the elders and those who upheld tribal institutions.

Waiyaki saw the meeting. He saw the converts gather and praise. All this was visible from his hut, whose door faced the place. Waiyaki could not tell his own feelings concerning the open challenge. Maybe he was indifferent. After all, he himself loved some Christian teaching. The element of love and sacrifice agreed with his own temperament. The suffering of Christ in the Garden of Gethsemane and His agony on the tree had always moved him. But he did not want to betray the tribe. Yet had he not actually betrayed it? He had wanted to bridge the gulf between Joshua and the others. For what? He had not stopped to answer that question. The feeling that this was in a way his mission had come to him before the meeting that marked the height of his glory. And he had been training himself for this mission: end the Kameno-Makuyu feud and bring back the unity of the tribe. Yet when the appropriate moment came he had failed. He had become intoxicated with wonder, anger and surprise and had lost himself. The moment had come. The moment had passed. Had he remained calm he would have spoken outright for reconciliation.

'Another time. Next time,' Waiyaki always told himself when these moments of self-blame came. And in a way he was glad. Education was really his mission. This was his passion. He needed help and co-operation from all, even from Joshua and Kabonyi. They called him a saviour. His own father had talked of a Messiah to come. Whom was the Messiah coming to save? From what? And where would He lead the people? Although Waiyaki did not stop to get clear answers to these questions, he increasingly saw himself as the one who would lead the tribe to the light. Education was the light of the country. That was what the people wanted. Education. Schools. Education. He did not see any connection between what his education mission and what the Kiama was doing. He just wanted all the people to get learning. And unity was the answer. But sometimes he was afraid. Joshua and his followers were now completely identified with the white man. And now, with this outright boldness of Joshua, this naked challenge, he could not tell what would happen. What would the Kiama do? He had resigned from the Kiama, and he did not know what the inner circle under the leadership of Kabonyi would be up to; in a way it controlled the secrets of the hills. Kamau had taken Waiyaki's place. His name had in fact been suggested by Waiyaki. Was this an act of appeasement? Waiyaki did not know. All he wanted was to concentrate his attention and energy on the mission he had undertaken. The Kiama could look to the purity of the tribe.

Again Waiyaki watched and saw the Christian gathering. He was much interested in this human spectacle. A thought came to him. Nyambura might be there. His heart beat a little. He always felt excited at the thought of seeing her. The more he thought of her the more he knew that he loved her. This was strange for Waiyaki. He had never shown much interest in women, his whole idea of living and purpose in life being concentrated on the service to the tribe. Though they met rarely, each time he was with her he wanted to tell. But he thought that she would turn on him and shame him to himself. No. He could

**101**

never risk this. There was a gulf between them. And he always felt foolish while he stood in front of her.

Waiyaki left his hut and went out, taking the opposite direction, leading away from the meeting place. After a distance he turned to the left and began walking towards Honia river. A group of people going towards Kameno passed near him and went on. They were going to the meeting. Again he turned to the left and began walking along the river. The sun was not very high in the sky. The shadows of trees were long and crossed one another. Honia river flowed on, on. Waiyaki moved slowly, yet as if he were going to a definite place. Suddenly he stopped short. His heart gave two quick beats. He had seen Nyambura.

Nyambura was not happy. Each day that she spent in her father's home seemed a greater weight added on to her. Her heart was restless and she knew that nothing at home would satisfy her. Every day she thought more and more of Waiyaki, her happy moments being those when she was with him. She was proud of his fame and at times she felt as if she shared it. She nursed this in her heart and clung to it as if the fame were hers. Yet his name, like Muthoni's, was never mentioned in her home. But she always longed to see him, to hear his voice. They had met on so few occasions and always by accident. Why could she not feel free to meet him anywhere, free to go out and see him? Day by day she became weary of Joshua's brand of religion. Was she too becoming a rebel? No. She would not do as her sister had done. She knew, however, that she had to have a God who would give her a fullness of life, a God who would still her restless soul; so she clung to Christ because He had died on the Tree, love for all the people blazing out from His sad eyes. She wished He could be near her so that she might wash and dress His wounds. She envied Mary, the Mary who had anointed the feet of Christ with oil. She prayed to Him. He must not leave her. Even this did not always satisfy her and she hungered for somebody human to talk to; somebody whom she could actually touch and feel and not a Christ who died many years ago, a Christ who could only talk to her in the spirit. If only she could meet Waiyaki more often; if only he could stay near her, then Christ would have a bigger meaning for her. But Waiyaki was becoming important and he was on the other side. Perhaps they would remain like that, a big, deep valley separating them. Nyambura knew then that she could never be saved by Christ; that the Christ who died could only be meaningful if Waiyaki was there for her to touch, for her to feel and talk to. She could only be saved through Waiyaki. Waiyaki then was her Saviour, her black Messiah, the promised one who would come and lead her into the light.

Muthoni said she had seen Jesus. She had done so by going back to the tribe, by marrying the rituals of the tribe with Christ. And she had seen Him through suffering. She had been circumcised and said she had become a woman. Nyambura too wanted to become a woman but she could only be so if Waiyaki talked to her, if he stood near her. Then she would see Christ.

Nyambura lived with her doubts. She would not recognize her feelings towards Waiyaki as love. She told herself she did not love him because she did not feel towards him as she felt towards her mother or Muthoni. But she saw him as something big, firm and sure. If the earth collapsed, she could hold on to him and be safe.

Sometimes she cried and asked God to forgive her. She still wanted to remain true to her father. She would obey him. After all, Waiyaki was too far away from her. And he did not care for her. He was a Teacher, a big leader. The only objects of his efforts were the many children all over the country who were now going to school. What then? Would such a man care for her, a man who had big things to think about? Would such a man associate himself with a girl who was not circumcised, a girl whose father led the other side? At such times she prayed that she might be true to her father. It was good for her to stay with him, to obey him instead of venturing into the dark unknown.

Nevertheless she was wearied. And going to church was becoming a burden to her, especially in the company of her father. So she was always left behind and she would walk slowly, slowly. Sometimes she would not go to church at all and instead she would go to the Honia river. There she would find peace. There she prayed to God and remembered her sister.

Today she had felt depressed. She would not go to the meeting till she had passed through her favourite spot. She did not find any peace. But she knelt down, and while the river murmured down its course she prayed with all her heart that she might find the peace and light she longed for.

A pleasurable numbness dulled Waiyaki into immobility. He did not move but leaned against a tree and watched the apparition. The girl was on the opposite bank, in a flat clearing hidden a little by small bushes. Waiyaki could not tell why the place reminded him so much of the sacred grove where long ago his father had taken him and revealed the ancient prophecy. This place she was in was sacred too. Nyambura seemed to be bending over something. And Waiyaki watched, held by the desire to possess her. He moved a little. He could now see her clearly. She was kneeling down in a praying posture. He was fascinated. A kind of holy light seemed to emanate from her body. The place would for ever remain sacred to him. A few yards away from here was the place where he had sat long ago when being circumcised. It was the place where he had shed blood, red blood, as if it were needed to propitiate angry spirits. When Waiyaki realized she was praying he was moved. It was very strange and as he watched he experienced a frightening sensation, as if she and he were together standing on an altar ready for a sacrifice.

A grave atmosphere seemed to envelop the whole area and Waiyaki wanted to go away. He would not see her. No. Not now. All he wanted was to run away from this, for he could not face it. He was confronted with a might, a presence far beyond him. And he now felt her beyond him, on the other side. He made as if to move away, unseen. But the dry crack of a broken twig betrayed him. She raised her head and saw him. Waiyaki stood and looked at her. Nyambura still knelt. Their eyes met

104

and they did not utter a word. Nyambura was afraid of the intense excitement that possessed her. Then Waiyaki made as if to move again, now feeling afraid of her, as if the intense glare in her eyes would destroy him. He wanted to shake off that power she now exercised over him on this altar of sacrifice. But her excitement was growing to a breaking point and she spoke to him, forcing herself to be calm. A note of defiance and challenge was discernible in the voice. And Waiyaki saw that she had been crying.

'Don't run away, Teacher,' she said.

A pleasant shock went through Waiyaki and made his body hot with desire. She had actually called him 'Teacher', a name no follower of Joshua would call him. Was there a mocking laughter in the voice? He could not tell. He waited for her patiently.

'Where are you going?' she asked him when she had crossed the river. Waiyaki felt confused. The question wrung the truth out of him. He had wanted to go round and sit in a place where he could watch the meeting at a distance ... the hope of seeing her.

'I was just walking. I like the river, the bush and the trees.'

'I am going to the meeting.'

'I thought you would already be there. It was a surprise to see you.'

'I – I just wanted to pass through here.' A pause. Then she laughed, a little nervously. 'You see, I also like the river, the bush and the trees. That is my favourite spot.'

'Do you often come here?'

'Sometimes I do. Not very often.'

Waiyaki was quiet. Another silence fell between them. His whole body was on fire.

'My sister was initiated there.' She said abruptly. She made him feel guilty.

'You still remember her—'

'How can I forget her? I loved her.'

'Were you only two in your family?'

'Yes; now I am alone.'

'I am also alone in my family. All my sisters are married. The youngest, whom I loved most, died a long time ago. I was then young—'

Nyambura felt pleased because of this exchange of confidence. Waiyaki did not know what else to say.

'You will be late for the meeting.'

She did not move. Then quietly, as if speaking to herself, she said, 'She was brave, very brave. Do you remember her?'

'I do, always.'

'Her last words.'

'Yes. . . .'

And Waiyaki's mind went back to that scene a few years back when they had carried Muthoni to Siriana. And he remembered her frail body, her black shining eyes, and her last message: 'Tell Nyambura I see Jesus.' Now he could see her again, clearly. And he remembered her agony. Waiyaki always felt that Muthoni had found something, something that filled her soul and made her endure everything. Muthoni had tried to find salvation for herself, a surer ground on which to stand. Where did *he* stand? The yearning came back to him, expressing itself in slow but mounting waves of desire. And he fixed his eyes on Nyambura and for a moment thought he could see Muthoni the night when they had met in the darkness on the eve of the initiation. He took a step towards Nyambura and stood close to her. He took her right hand in his and at once burst out, 'Nyambura, I love you.'

It was really a whisper. Nyambura saw the light in his eyes and for a second she was afraid; she could not believe her ears. But it was good that he loved her. She wanted to fall into his arms, still she feared. And now she felt a painful sorrow come into her heart as if from nowhere. A tear dropped down her left cheek. She did not try to hold it back and a second fell down the right cheek. Waiyaki pressed her hand and she returned the pressure so, that he felt he would die. In a blind moment of passion he took her into his arms and pressed her close to his breast while tears from her eyes fell on to his shoulder. Nyambura did not resist but allowed herself to be held by him, the

106

only man who could save her from her misery. Neither spoke. They were one. Waiyaki thought his quest was over.

'Will you marry me?' he whispered.

Nyambura rested on his broad breast. She wanted to say 'Yes'. She longed to say this. It would cost her nothing. Only her breath. Slowly she came to her senses. She disengaged herself from him. She was no longer crying.

'Tell me, oh, tell me,' implored Waiyaki, hope and fear mixing together. There was another silence.

'No,' she said at last faintly.

It cost her a lot of effort to whisper this. But she knew she had to. It was impossible to marry him. Unless she rebelled. She didn't want to rebel like her sister. Waiyaki felt hurt.

'Why? Don't you love me?'

'I do, I do,' her heart said. 'But can't you see we cannot marry? Can't you?' Aloud she said, 'Father will not allow it. I cannot disobey him. He knows that we have met before. Through rumours.'

He was looking aside now and could not see the tears that flowed freely down her face. If she continued, she would sob. It was better for them to part. But she wanted him and it was painful to her that she had to leave. Quickly she moved away before it was too late. She left him standing in the same position, staring at the same place. It pained her all the more and she stood irresolutely. She knew she had to go.

'Nyambura! Nyambura!' Oh, she was gone. What had he wanted to tell her? He retraced his steps and went home, seeing nothing, feeling nothing. He just walked.

Kamau came out of his hiding place. His eyes and soul burnt with malice. He'll suffer for this. And his accumulated fury rose against Waiyaki. Kamau had never forgotten that incident when Waiyaki had humiliated him in the plains. He would never forget the wound. Kamau knew that he hated Waiyaki. He was now known as the Teacher. Some said he would save the hills. Well, let him be their Teacher. Let him be their saviour. Kamau rejected him. This man had humiliated his father. Would Kamau after all these things stand aside and watch Waiyaki beat him in love? No. Kamau loved Nyambura. He had always wanted her and in Makuyu he always hovered around, hoping one day to declare his love to her. Yet he had never had a good chance to open his heart to her. Today had been an excellent opportunity. He had meant to do it. He would have told her all about himself and he was sure that she would have agreed to run away with him to Nairobi. Then this fool had come. Kamau had waited for him to go but Waiyaki had persisted in staying. Then he saw them embrace. And with intense pain he saw all he had half feared confirmed before his eyes. Waiyaki was his rival to death.

# CHAPTER TWENTY

Waiyaki went from ridge to ridge, meeting elder after elder. They came to him and felt comforted by the blaze in his eyes. He had a passion to live for. His god, education, guided him, showed him the light, made him overcome personal frustrations and hardships. It drove him through hills and valleys, through the forests and darkness of the night. He had not yet stopped to think where all this was leading, whether the new awareness and enthusiasm he had helped to create would be quenched by education. If anybody had suddenly asked him a question in that direction, he might have burst out: Unite and build more schools.

But just now he was faced with the task of getting more teachers for the schools already built. Something had to be done. Again Siriana was the only place which could still produce men with the necessary education for carrying on the teaching in the ridges. So he one day made a sudden journey to a ridge near Siriana, where he met some young men who were in their final year at the Mission place. He talked to them and pleaded with them. They agreed to his proposals but asked him to go back before Christmas Day to straighten out the arrangement.

At home the Kiama was getting more and more power over the people. The cry that started the new schools was again taken up. Keep the tribe pure. And people listened to them because they did not want the tribe to die. And the Kiama wanted to fight for the land which had now been taken by the settler, the missionary and the government. Kabonyi and his followers went from ridge to ridge, getting people to take the oath of allegiance to the purity of the tribe. People knew that their Teacher had taken such an oath. And he had been one of the leaders of the Kiama, at least before he resigned. Nobody could break this oath. Nobody who had taken it would ever betray the tribe.

The old rivalry went on. And it was spreading to the other ridges. Joshua's centre was Makuyu, while Kameno was seen as the centre of the tribe. The Teacher came from there. Waiyaki did not like to be identified with either side; he was now committed to reconciliation. But since those two memorable meetings things had gone from bad to worse. Each group seemed more arrogant and more confident of itself than ever. Joshua preached with more vigour than ever and his followers sang damnation to the pagans openly and defiantly. Joshua was identified as the enemy of the tribe. He was with Siriana, with the white settlers. For now it was said that Siriana missionaries had been sent to prepare the way for the settlers. The white people were now pouring into the interior in greater and greater numbers. Indian traders too had come and were beginning to carry on a thriving business.

For Waiyaki the fleeting feeling of guilt at having failed to preach reconciliation was now growing stronger. He had missed the opportunity at a time when he could have made his stand clear. A combination of events, excitement and Kabonyi had made him lose that moment when he had the people from the various ridges under control. Would such a chance come again? He would bide his time. He would wait for another moment, a moment when he would preach reconciliation, tolerance and unity. Then his work would be done. His mission of enlightenment through education would prosper. Early next year there would be another conference of the parents. Then he would speak his mind.

Waiyaki continued working hard day by day. The moments of self-blame came to him these days with greater and greater vigour and persistence. But he had still his joy when an old man, a women or a child stopped him and shook hands with him, a smile of trust on their faces. He was thankful that he had left the Kiama. He would not have been able to carry on its activities and those of the new schools' committee.

He often thought of Nyambura. It pained him that she had

refused him. Often he tried to whistle the whole thing off. He could only do this by throwing himself into activity.

Kinuthia came to him after school. He came with an air of secrecy.

'I would like to talk with you.'

'You have never warned me before whenever you want to speak with me.'

'Please do not laugh so,' Kinuthia begged him. 'I think it is serious.'

'What?'

'What I heard. Is it true?'

'You have not told me anything about it. I am in the dark.' Waiyaki could see that something serious weighed heavily on Kinuthia. Now Kinuthia seemed embarrassed.

'You have, er . . .' There was a pause. In that pause Waiyaki felt the silence in the school. The children had gone home and Kamau, with a new teacher who had joined Marioshoni, had left.

'Waiyaki said. 'I am still waiting.'

'You have become one of Joshua's followers.'

'Me? Who says so?'

'Nobody really, perhaps it's a joke. You know, for example, how our people like rumours. A few people have been talking here and there. Well, it is said that you have been seen in Joshua's church many times.'

'I have been there once. But what is wrong in going there?'

'Not only that. It is said that some months ago you went to Siriana and you had a long talk with the white men there. You want to sell the people.'

Waiyaki laughed. He knew he need not take it seriously. There was nothing in it but rumours. That must have been the time he went to see the young men near Siriana about teaching in the ridges. So he said, 'Well?'

'And . . .'

Waiyaki looked up. There was a change in the voice of Kinuthia.

'Let's go and sit on the grass.'

They moved in silence and sat on a grassy spot in front of the school.

'Is it true that you are intending to marry Joshua's daughter?' Kinuthia asked as soon as they had sat down.

Waiyaki almost jumped. This came to him as a surprise. He had not met Nyambura since that day. And again the memory of her refusal came back, numbing him. This was irony. That people should talk of his possible marriage to Nyambura when she had in fact refused him! And Kinuthia was talking with great excitement.

'Be careful, Waiyaki. You know the people look up to you. You are the symbol of the tribe, born again with all its purity. They adore you. They worship you. You do not know about the new oath. You have been too busy. But they are taking the new oath in your name. In the name of the Teacher and the purity of the tribe. And remember Kabonyi hates, hates you. He would kill you if he could. And he is the one who is doing all this. Why? The Kiama has power. Power. And your name is in it, giving it even greater power. Your name will be your ruin. Be careful. . . .'

Kinuthia was very excited. His voice was full of concern and anxiety. Waiyaki laid his hand on Kinuthia.

'It is all right. She would not marry me. And they would not do anything to me.'

'There are young men there. I know them. They are loyal to Kabonyi. And they are sworn to keep the tribe pure and punish betrayal. . . .'

'I tell you, she would not marry me.'

'So it is true?'

'What?'

'That you'll marry her?'

'Listen, Kinuthia. I tell you, she would not accept me.'

He went to see an elder a few weeks after this. The elder was a close associate of Kabonyi. The old man talked about Waiyaki's own father and grandfather. He praised them for their

112

bravery. He ended by saying that they never would have betrayed the tribe. Waiyaki went home his heart glowing with pride. His ancestors had done well.

But at night it suddenly occurred to him that the old man hinted a warning to him. What made Waiyaki connect this warning and Kinuthia's information? Yet the more he thought about it, the more it all seemed to become clear.

Christmas was approaching. This season of the year coincided with the coming tribal ceremonies and rituals. Waiyaki did not take part in them as much as he used to do. His work was becoming almost more than he could manage. Many teachers from all over the ridge came to see him, and many elders and children came to him with various problems. But in spite of all this Waiyaki was losing that contact with people that can only come through taking part together in a ritual. He was becoming too obsessed with the schools and the widening rift and divisions.

Then it happened. It was a thing that scared everyone. Such a thing had never happened before. A hut that belonged to one of Joshua's newest followers was burnt. Nobody was hurt but everything that was in the hut was destroyed. Waiyaki could not tell why, but he connected the incident with the Kiama. Was Kabonyi determined to destroy all that stood against him and the tribe?

The realization came to him as a shock. He instantly thought that he should not have resigned from the Kiama. Its power and influence was there, everywhere.

# CHAPTER TWENTY-ONE

When the service was over, Nyambura went home to prepare food for her father. He came with some other people. Nyambura could not rest. After she had given them something to eat, she went out.

She did not know what she wanted to do or where she wanted to go. All she wanted was to be alone. She had never been the same since she rejected Waiyaki's offer of marriage. She kept her outward calmness. At home she did her small jobs as usual. But she was becoming more irritable and often resented her father's commands. She wanted to live over again the moment when she stood in Waiyaki's arms feeling that all was well. She had often prayed that Waiyaki should come to her, should love her and save her from misery. That had almost happened. He loved her. But she could not marry him. It was the thought that she was the one who had refused him which most troubled her. Would he understand? She feared that she might never see him again.

Why had she said 'No' when she would have been happier saying 'Yes'? She loved him. She wanted him. He was her only saviour. Yet when he came to her she had run away from him. It was difficult for her to rebel against her father. He was always there, at the back of her, a weight, a conscience that showed her only one way to follow. But it was a way she did not want to follow. She now wished to rebel. Muthoni had done it. Nyambura had not Muthoni's courage. And so the struggle went on in her heart. At one time she would want to go to seek Waiyaki out and ask him to take her again. She would whisper to him, 'Waiyaki, I love you.' At other times she would fight against her feelings for him and she would feel proud that she had stuck to her father. She was not sure if Joshua had so far heard about her being seen with Waiyaki. She never understood why she had told Waiyaki a lie. 'He knows we have met. . . .' Yet she was convinced it was not a lie. She had always had a feeling that Joshua knew. It could be the way he looked at her, or it could be the way he twisted his preaching to remind her and others of the absolute necessity of keeping away from pagans, however learned. And then a few days before she met Waiyaki her mother had spoken to her privately. 'Waiyaki is a good young man. But people can talk, you know. We do not want any more trouble in this house. I cannot bear it. Not after Muthoni . . .' Another woman had just then called on them and so Nyambura had not had a chance of hearing all that her mother had to say.

Nyambura knew that her mother liked Waiyaki. For Miriamu had never forgotten that it was Waiyaki who had showed most concern at the plight of Muthoni. It was he who had taken her to the hospital. Every night she prayed to Christ that Waiyaki might find salvation and come to their side.

Nyambura went to her usual place by Honia river. Her heart beat fast as she came near the place. It was there, there in the forest, that she had stood and rested in his arms. It was there that she had heard from his own lips that he loved her. She thought that he might still be there waiting for her. She crossed the river and tore through the bush, hoping, praying that Waiyaki might be there. Would she tell him that now she was ready, ready to marry him and go to live with him for ever?

But she knew he would not be there. After all, she had not been to the place since they had parted. Still, it hurt her that he was not there. Her heart accused him of unfaithfulness. Surely he ought to come and see her. He must come again. Now. Her misery mingled with despair and she felt she could hate him. Of course it was all ridiculous. And inside her she was accusing herself for having rejected him.

She went back to the opposite bank and sat in her favourite spot. To her left was open ground where the candidates for circumcision went to shed their blood. Muthoni too had come here on the morning of her sacrifice. Nyambura did not feel at peace. The river no longer soothed her.

When the evening came and the birds began to fly away, Nyambura went home. Joshua was there standing at the door. She did not like the way he looked at her. Something was wrong. He let her enter without saying a word to her. Miriamu was inside and she too did not speak to Nyambura. Her father followed her in.

'Where have you been?' His voice was menacing. She was afraid of him.

'Near the river.'

'Who was with you?'

'I was alone, Father.' She was trembling. She had gone to the river hoping that her saviour would come in a cloud and rescue her. But Waiyaki had not come. Her obedience to her father had made her lose him.

'No one?'

'Yes.'

'You are lying. You are lying.'

'I was alone, Father,' she insisted.

'Do not think I am blind. I am not that old. And don't you cheat yourself I have not heard things. If I hear that you have been seen with that young devil again you will no longer live in this house.'

'I have been alone,' she burst out, almost crying.

'I'll tell you again. If you are seen with him once more – have they not done enough harm to this house? And don't you remember how they burnt the hut of a man of God?'

'But—'

'Let me catch you! Let me catch you with him again.' There was more than malice in that voice.

Nyambura did not say anything else. This was her reward for being true and obedient to him. And because of her obedience she had lost the one man whom she loved. And with him her salvation. That night she could not sleep. She wept all the time, praying that God should kill her.

# CHAPTER TWENTY-TWO

And now they sang his praises in every hill. He had got them teachers and their children would drink the learning they yearned for from these new wells. After all, what were schools without teachers? That had been everybody's worry since the last great meeting. They had trusted Waiyaki to do something but even then some people had their doubts. Teachers could only be got from the claws of Siriana. Waiyaki had done it.

Kinuthia now almost worshipped Waiyaki. He felt he could serve under him for ever. This was an unusual man, he told the elders whom he met. And the elders agreed and nodded with secret knowledge. Waiyaki was the son of Chege, they whispered. They knew that Chege had been a great man. Even in his youth he had said strange things that others could not quite comprehend. Kinuthia still retained his strong political views and was one of the people who believed in 'Action Now'. That was why in a way he admired Kabonyi and his Kiama. These too believed in action against the white man. But the Great Teacher's vision of a highly learned people carried him along. How could he resist the power of that vision, unrolled before him in Waiyaki's slow but powerful voice? Not only the voice. The eyes, too, carried the vision and Kinuthia knew that Waiyaki believed in this mission. He feared for him because he could see some things that seemed hidden to Waiyaki. He could, for instance, recognize that Kabonyi's hatred of Waiyaki had turned into a mission, a mission that had the strength of a political conviction which was an integral part of Kabonyi's vision of freedom of the ridges.

When Waiyaki came back from his second trip to Siriana and told the good news to the inter-ridge schools' committee, Kinuthia felt a warmth of pride and joy in his heart. He felt small as he walked beside Waiyaki.

'Will they all come from Kiambu?'

'No! Some will come from Kabete, Muranga and Nairobi. They mean to help us for they too in a way are tired of Siriana. They want to help in these Gikuyu independent schools.'

Kinuthia and Waiyaki walked along Honia river in silence. Waiyaki was overwhelmed by the warmth and enthusiasm with which his news had been received by the elders. Kinuthia looked at Waiyaki's contracted face. He said. 'When they come we must present them to the gathering of parents next year.'

'Yes, yes, we shall.' And then, suddenly, Waiyaki turned to Kinuthia. 'We must build up the hills. We must capture this enthusiasm. We must build schools . . . and a college, a great big college. . . .'

Kinuthia was moved not so much by the words as by the way in which Waiyaki said them. There was fire and conviction in them. Yet he wondered if Waiyaki knew that people wanted action now, that the new enthusiasm and awareness embraced more than the mere desire for learning. People wanted to move forward. They could not do so as long as their lands were taken, as long as their children were forced to work in the settled ridges, as long as their women and men were forced to pay hut-tax. He did not want to tell this now, but he would tell him. One day. For Kinuthia was convinced that Waiyaki was the best man to lead people, not only to a new light through education, but also to new opportunities and areas of self-expression through political independence. Waiyaki was the best man to lead the Kiama. Even now his spirit was responsible for the power the Kiama and Kabonyi exercised on the people. Did Waiyaki know this? As Kinuthia beheld the fire in the Teacher's eyes, he wondered if the vision of a new light had not blinded him. But he believed in him and he wanted to share in this vision and share in the task of its fulfilment.

Kinuthia, however, did not know the extent of Waiyaki's dreams and vision. How could he know unless he entered those regions of the heart where doubts and fears struggled in the darkness, where you suddenly lost sight of your hopes and success, shaken to the roots as you woke up at night, or even as you walked along the paths in the country?

As Waiyaki lay in bed two days later, he felt exhausted in body and spirit. He felt as if something evil lurked a few feet behind him, following the path of his success, ready to pounce on him and reduce him to nothing. This was not fear or even despair. It was just a feeling that hovered around him, making him weary. And yet he clung to his vision and let its light illuminate the path ahead. Ever since the burning of the hut a few days before he left for Siriana, he had been thinking more and more intensely about his people. He looked forward to the day early next year when the parents would gather again, when he would tell them all to unite. But unite for what?

To Waiyaki the white man's education was an instrument of enlightenment and advance if only it could be used well. He still remembered his father's words, that long time ago, when they stood on a hill, the whole country before them:

'Learn all the wisdom and all the secrets of the white man. But do not follow his vices.'

Was this then his mission to the ridges? He would tell the people. Indeed he had already told them. The children must learn.

'A man shall rise and save the people in their hour of need.'

Was he that saviour? Was he the Promised One or had Chege's mind been roving? How would he save them? Chege had placed a burden on his shoulders, a burden hard to carry. A saviour did something big, something that had power to change the lives of the people. A saviour did something startling, a thing that happened so suddenly one night that nobody could resist its power. What had he himself done?

But now he wanted an opportunity to shout what was oppressing his mind. He would tell the people – 'Unite'. That would be early next year. For a moment he dreamt the dream. It was a momentary vision that flashed across his mind and seemed to light the dark corners of his soul. It was the vision of a people who could trust one another, who would sit side by side, singing the song of love which harmonized with music from the birds, and all their hearts would beat to the rhythm of the throbbing river. The children would play there, jumping from rock on to rock, splashing the water which reached fathers and mothers sitting in the shade around, talking, watching. Birds sang as they hovered from tree to tree, while farther out in the forest beasts of the land circled around. . . . In the midst of this Nyambura would stand. The children would come to her and she would talk to the elders. The birds too seemed to listen and even the beasts stopped moving and stood still. And a song rose stirring the hearts of all, and their longing for a new life in the future was reflected in the dark eyes of Nyambura.

He stretched his hands and wanted to touch her trembling figure as she led them into this song. And then he saw that the hands of the other people, including Joshua, were stretched towards her. For a moment he stood still, fascinated by the sight. And then horror caught him. They were all pulling her into pieces, as if she were a thing of sacrifice to the god of the river, which still flowed with life as they committed this ritual outrage on her. And he too had joined the crowd and he was tearing her to himself and she did not cry out because she was now dumb. Then he saw that it was Muthoni, and she was thrown into the river and she was saying, 'I am a woman now.' The river carried her with it into a darkness which no one could fathom. Waiyaki's heart cried and he knew that she was not there. She had gone. And everybody turned away, not speaking to one another because they felt guilty. They averted their eyes from Waiyaki, the Teacher, as they passed him. At last he was left alone. He did not know whether he should follow Muthoni or the crowd. Nyambura now stood in front of him. A flash of joy drove the guilt away and he went forward to touch her. She would not let him. And Waiyaki wanted to remonstrate with her and remind her of that one time when she had allowed him to hold her in his arms. But he remembered that Nyambura had not agreed to marry him. Why did she refuse? Because she would not disobey a father? Yes. That was the word. Obedience. And because she was obedient he had lost her. For ever. And his yearning would go on, on, till he died. Death was the end of everything. He was about to open his mouth and tell her that Joshua had led the crowd in tearing her to pieces. Then Waiyaki remembered that he too had chosen the crowd, had acceded to the ritual demands of the tribe and had shed her blood. Guilt weighed on him. The darkness terrified him. He wanted to scream in horror of himself. He had failed to tell people to unite. Another time. A next time. And he woke up still panting, next time.

Waiyaki shook himself out of the terror of that vision. He was sure that he had not fallen asleep. He felt his face and it was full of sweat. He looked around the hut. It was not late really. He was only tired and he wanted to rest. But now he knew that he could not sleep. The image that had transfixed him to his bed was too real for him to shake himself from its effect.

He wished he could have taken a more active part in the ceremonial activities of the tribe. That, at least, would have given him more comfort and made him feel still one of the people. But the journeys! Circumcision was coming soon, hardly a week away. The initiation day would coincide with Christmas Day. Was this a challenge to Joshua? Dancing and singing was in full swing. And there was a new edge to the songs. Uncircumcised girls were the objects of cutting attacks. Everything dirty and impure was heaped on them. They were the impure things of the tribe and they would bring the wrath of the ancestral spirits on the ridges. A day would come when all these *Irigu* would be circumcised by force, to rid the land of all impurities. Joshua and his followers took up the challenge. They sang of Christ and His saving power. They sang of a Child who was born in Bethlehem, who was put in a manger and had swaddling clothes.

It was no good sleeping early. He could not do it. He got out of bed and went to his mother's hut. He wanted to go out into the village and talk to the elders or other men of his *riika*. For the next few days, he told himself, he would lose himself in the

life of the ridge. If he had lost Nyamura, he had not lost his
faith in service to the community.

His mother had not yet gone to bed. She was now very old
and she sat near the fireplace. Waiyaki felt his conscience prick
him. He had kept away from her for a long time. He thought,
'I'll marry soon so that she can have a companion.' Then a fear
suddenly gripped him. Perhaps he would never marry. Waiyaki
felt as if he would fall on his aged mother and let her comfort
him as on that day when she had soothed him during his
second birth. The feeling came and went. He was again calm.
He did not want to stay long with his mother and so he rose to
go.

'Where are you going, son?' She did not raise her eyes.

'Out, Mother.'

She now looked at him, at his strange eyes which spoke of an
inner agitation. 'Waiyaki.'

He turned round sharply, fearfully. His mother stared at him
in the eyes. There was a strange tremor in her voice.

'Is it true that you are marrying Joshua's daughter?'

The rumours! Spreading like fire in a plain of dry grass. This
talk about marrying Nyambura annoyed him. Had she not
refused him? She was obedient to her father. Waiyaki wondered what he should tell his mother. Should he tell her that he
loved Nyambura? He thought of her. She had betrayed him. If
only she had agreed! If only he had a hope! Then maybe he
would be in a position to face any challenge. He would have
known what to say when a person confronted him with a question like this. And he hated her. She had taken the path of duty.
He too would take the path of duty and stick to the tribe. His
father had warned him of contaminating the tribe with the
white man's ways, had warned him not to betray the tribe.
Would an association with Nyambura not be a betrayal? He
would not stand by her. He would not take her part. And he
would not trouble his mother with an explanation. So Waiyaki
only said one word: 'No!'

And immediately he hated himself. Surely he ought to tell
her all. He ought to tell his mother of his secret yearning, of his

122

strong love for Nyambura. She was a mother. She surely could know of a cure. But when he opened his mouth, the words refused to form. Only a light shone in his eyes.

His mother went on in her weak voice, 'You know what this would mean. You must not do it. Fear the voice of the Kiama. It is the voice of the people. When the breath of the people turns against you, it is the greatest curse you can ever get.'

Waiyaki now knew that it would be futile for him to explain. She would not understand. In her eyes such a relationship with a girl who was not circumcised would be a betrayal.

There was a knock at the door. Kamau entered.

'Is it well with you all?'

'It is well,' Waiyaki answered, glad of the interruption.

'The elders and the Kiama want to see you.'

Waiyaki had not been invited to appear before the Kiama since his resignation. He looked at his mother, whose eyes seemed imploring and plainly saying 'Don't go'. For a moment Waiyaki thought she was not well. He felt it his duty to be with her but he now welcomed this chance to talk to the Kiama and come to an understanding with them. If the mission thrust on to him by his father was going to succeed, he had to secure the co-operation of everyone. But he said, 'I think Mother is ill.'

'It is important that you be there. Were it not so, I would not have come at this hour. You'll only be away for a short time.'

'All right,' he said, avoiding the eyes of his mother.

And the two stepped out into the dark night.

# CHAPTER TWENTY-THREE

'Why does the Kiama want me?' Waiyaki asked again as soon as they had stepped out.

'Oh, I don't know exactly,' Kamau answered vaguely, yet with a note of finality that invited no more questions. Waiyaki's mind was behind with his mother. Then he remembered the frightening images that had passed through his mind while he had lain awake in bed. He looked around in the darkness and felt a terror of nothing visible pursue him.

'It is a dark night,' he commented.

'It is dark,' Kamau agreed. These two never held a long conversation together, not unless there was a third person. Kinuthia had always been the third person. Kamau saw in Waiyaki the hawk that always snatched his piece of meat when he himself was about to eat it. How would he ever rise or succeed as long as Waiyaki was in the way? He came to hate him. The hatred had grown slowly, gathering violence as the years dragged along. And yet Kamau felt more and more powerless to fight against Waiyaki. He could never quite rouse himself to the effort.

The lone hut to which they went was a distance from Kabonyi's group of mud huts. The outside was dimly lit by a small lantern that was put on a stone near the fireplace. In the fireplace were glowing pieces of wood which gave an oppressive warmth to the hut. Waiyaki was aware of figures lurking in the edges of darkness and he took them for the elders.

'Is it well with you all?'

'It is well.'

There was not the same warmth of response and they did not call him the Teacher, a title which was now his name. He sat on a stool and wondered what was coming.

It was Kabonyi who first spoke. He was old, very old, yet his

124

eyes had that glitter in them that made you think they were the only live things in him. But he had energy and you could detect this in his voice. He spoke about the ridges, the initiation ceremonies that were under preparation. Now this ancient custom was about to be ruined by certain impurities in the land. The disease in the ridges had started with Joshua. The death of Muthoni had been the first contamination.

'But that is not our fear. The trouble now comes because the impurity in Joshua has caught some in our midst. It is the hidden soul in your body that kills you.'

Here he looked at Waiyaki meaningfully. A numbness came over the Teacher as he heard Kabonyi speak. He did not know where the talk was leading, but he could guess. He remembered Kinuthia's warning, the elder's hints and his own mother's questions. Waiyaki thought: 'And all this while I have busied myself with the education of their children.' Something like bitterness began to eat into him. To hear Kabonyi speak in that voice you would never think that he had once been one of Joshua's followers.

'Yes,' Kabonyi repeated slowly. There was a strange stillness in the hut. It was a stillness such as precedes a storm or an explosion. 'It is bad when he who has taken himself to be the leader of the people is touched by the impurity, for he is still in a position to spread the *thahu* to those close to him, to the stem and roots of the tribe. Such a person is a danger and he needs cleansing.'

Again Kabonyi paused, and his eyes rolled all round the hut, finally resting on Waiyaki. You could not tell if there was malice or scorn in that look. He spoke in an even voice and his words were measured.

'You, our Teacher, no doubt remember that girl, what was her name?'

'Which girl?' Waiyaki forced himself to ask. 'I am in the dark.'

'Joshua's daughter. Her name? Yes. Muthoni. She was not clean. Yet you took her to the hospital. You touched a dying woman, a dead body. And were you ever cleansed? I do not

**125**

think so. But you ought to have been. You are not ignorant and you know what this means to the tribe.'

Waiyaki was going to speak, but Kabonyi waved him into silence.

'I have not finished. That is the first thing you have done to the tribe. It is not a small thing. Then you were not a teacher, a person to whom we entrusted our children. But since you rose into the position in which you are, you have deliberately worked against the tribe. How many times have you been in Joshua's church? How many? No, wait, you have also been to Siriana. How many times? We know of two. You never told anybody that you were going there. Do you expect us to believe that you went to get teachers? Do you? You'll have to tell us of any secret dealings between you, Joshua and Siriana. Will you sell us to the white man? You see how restless and impatient our people are. They cry for a leader to save them from slavery. And you, you, who ought to have led them—'

'Stop!' Waiyaki shouted with anger. Then he realized that he ought not to shout at a man much older than himself. 'I don't know what you are talking about.' He tried to regulate his voice with difficulty. He wanted to rise and cry, 'You fool, you fool!' But he felt weary. He writhed within and remained stuck to his seat.

Another elder was speaking. It was the same elder who had dropped hints to Waiyaki a few weeks back.

'Betrayal. Betrayal is a bad thing for a man in a position of influence. The curse of the people falls on him. You elders will remember Nganyira. He was a great warrior. He led the tribe. But what happened? He was tempted by a Masai woman. He betrayed the tribe's secrets to the enemy. The curse of the people destroyed him. I could mention Wangira—' He added a few more names of those who had been unfaithful to the tribe and were in the end caught by the wrath of the people.

'That is why we warn you today. That is why you must tell us the truth. Are you marrying Joshua's daughter or not? For unless we know the position how can we entrust our secrets to

**126**

you? How can we know they will not later reach the white man?'

Yes. At last it had come. Yet he ought to have known. He was now on trial at Makuyu and he did not feel that he wanted to defend himself. Yet he spoke, forcing himself to remain calm.

'Elders. I did not know that such accusations based on rumours could ever reach me from your mouths. I am young. I think that youth should be led and where we go wrong, you, our fathers can and should correct us. Yet I see there is something more than the desire to correct in these accusations. I took Muthoni to the hospital. Because she was ill. I could never have let her die if I was in a position to help. I am not the person who initiated her. If she was unclean, why did the elders not object to her initiation? When she died, I did not touch her.

'As for Siriana, I can only tell you that I have never entered into any negotiation with the white man. I had gone there to try and get teachers for our schools which you agreed to build. There is no secret dealing between me and Joshua. I have never spoken to him.'

'What about going to his church?' Kabonyi asked.

'What has that got to do with anybody?' Waiyaki asked, anger getting the better of his calmness.

'It concerns the tribe, the people and their purity,' another elder put in.

Kabonyi and the Kiama were asking him to stand by their beliefs, beliefs that would destroy his mission of healing the rift between Makuyu and Kameno; between Joshua and the others. His mission of enlightenment through education would come to nothing. No! He could not be threatened into standing by Kabonyi. And if he came under the power of Kabonyi, all the work he had tried to do for the last few years would be annihilated. He must make his stand clear. Again he forced himself to remain calm.

'I too am concerned with the purity of the tribe. I am also concerned with the growth and development of the ridges. We cannot do this through hatred. We must be united, Christians and non-Christians, Makuyu or Kameno. For salvation of the hills lies in our hands.'

'Yet you would not fight the white man,' an elder interrupted.

'Our land is gone slowly, taken from us, while we and our young men sit like women, watching,' another elder put in.

'And we and our wives are forced to pay taxes,' still another followed.

'The schools, the schools,' Waiyaki pleaded with passion. 'We must know what the white man knows.'

'We need a leader.'

'A political leader.'

'Education—' Waiyaki started to say.

'Nothing. We need action now,' Kabonyi said triumphantly. 'But you have not yet replied to our worries. This girl – Joshua's daughter – you are marrying her?'

Waiyaki rose. He was now really exasperated. What had Nyambura got to do with them? What? Could he not do whatever he wanted with his own life? Or was his life not his own? He would tell them nothing about Nyambura.

'Nyambura has nothing to do with this. If I love her, I love her. If you have nothing else to tell me, I will go.'

'Remember the oath!'

'The oath!'

'You took it.'

'It did not forbid me to love people.'

'It forbids you to betray the tribe, to reveal its secrets, or to do anything unclean which might ruin us.'

He would not discuss Nyambura, a girl who had rejected him. He looked at Kabonyi. Hatred was all that the dimming light from the lantern could reveal. The gleam in Kamau's eyes spoke of silent triumph, and Waiyaki now knew that even Kamau hated him. Yet Waiyaki was more annoyed with himself, for he felt he had not put up a good fight. Maybe he had lost grip with the tribe. Maybe he did not know where he was leading them. As he left them and walked out the word 'traitor' followed him and he wondered if he had actually seen all the consequences of the awareness he had aroused in the hills. But bitterness and frustration mingled and drove him away. He felt angry with everybody, his own father, Nyambura, the elders, and with himself.

Kabonyi felt now triumphant as he faced the elders.

'Elders of the tribe. I told you. You would not believe me. He has not denied associating with Joshua or the white man. How can he continue to be a teacher? How can we go on following him? Where is he leading us?'

'He was always like that,' an elder said sadly.

'It is the girl. The girl has turned his mind the wrong way.'

'As we said earlier,' one more elder commented, 'all these Christians should be circumcised. By force.'

'Yes,' a few voices assented, but not all. For some feared that such an action would bring *thahu* to the land.

# CHAPTER TWENTY-FOUR

One evening a few days later Kinuthia burst into Waiyaki's hut. He looked worried and glanced back over his shoulder as if expecting some people to follow him.

'Waiyaki,' he breathed out.

'What is it, Kinuthia?' Waiyaki asked. He felt frightened. He had never seen Kinuthia like this before.

'What have they done?'

'Who?'

'The Kiama!'

'What?'

'They are spreading rumours that you are no longer a teacher.'

'Oh!'

There was a little silence. Waiyaki recovered from the momentary shock and said with a forced calmness, 'Please sit down. Where did you hear this?

'It is being whispered. You know how news spreads. Kamau told me the Kiama removed you from your job. You were in league with the white man.'

Waiyaki felt bitter that the elders for whom he had struggled should turn against him so.

'And how do the people take it?' he asked.

'I don't know. I think not all the people have heard. When did they do this to you?'

Waiyaki felt a sharp pain at the last question. He felt as if Kinuthia was one of the conspirators.

'To me? They cannot remove me from the job. It is not their responsibility. It is only the schools' committee who can do it. I really know nothing about this.'

Then he described to Kinuthia the events of the night he had been called to Makuyu.

'Perhaps I was wrong to let anger and passion get the better of me. The girl does not even love me.'

'This is all Kabonyi's doing. He hates you. Oh, you don't know how. Look, Waiyaki, I think something is happening to-night. Kamau hinted something about going to Joshua's household tonight. I don't know, but the young men might do something bad. They think it is Nyambura who has corrupted you.'

'Wait! What do they want to do?'

'I don't know. But I think it might be something rough. And they will not stop at that. They may come to you. For they say you have broken the oath. You have given away the secrets. So you must flee the land. Fly to Nairobi. I tell you again: Kabonyi is after you and he will get you. He has a new influence with the elders. They cannot resist his power. The man has no roots anywhere and he talks of an ancient proph-ecy about a saviour. He is that saviour, he says. . . .'

Waiyaki rose. He remembered that Chege had told him that it was only Kabonyi who knew of the ancient prophecy. Perhaps that was why Kabonyi hated him. But now he knew there was no time to lose. His mind was made up. He had to go and warn Joshua.

'Thank you, Kinuthia. But I must go.'

'Where?'

'To Makuyu. I must warn Joshua. Violence must not break out among the people. Oh, not now.'

'No, Teacher.'

'I must go.'

'But you cannot. They will have an excuse to try you as a traitor if they get to know of this.'

'Kinuthia.'

'Yes?'

'You remember you and I have grown up together.'

'Yes.' Kinuthia could remember more than Waiyaki could guess.

'Then do not stop me.' Waiyaki's voice was calm. 'Do not think that I am not grateful. I value your concern so much. You are the only man I can now trust. But we cannot allow this to happen to Joshua through the madness of one person. Maybe I have not done all that I should have done for the tribe. I do not want to bring you into this. Don't come with me. If you stay here I'll come back and we shall talk. I will tell you of my plans.'

Kinuthia did not argue. He could detect a firmness behind the calmness of Waiyaki. Yet he could still see that there was an agitation in the eyes of the Teacher. He let Waiyaki go. But he did not remain in the hut. He too went out and followed the Teacher up to Monia river.

Waiyaki climbed up the slopes, hoping fearfully that he might be in time to warn them. He tried to run up the ridge towards Joshua's house. He had never been there before. Even from afar, he could hear them singing.

> Maikarite thi Utuku
> Ariithi a Mburi
> Murekio wa Ngai niokire
> Nake akimera o uu.

> While shepherds watched their flocks by night
> All seated on the ground
> The angel of the Lord came down
> And glory shone around.

Indeed, Christmas was near. The Christians were keeping their watch by night like those shepherds of old.

When Waiyaki entered, breathless, everyone stopped and looked at him. To them he was a strange apparition. For a few minutes there was silence as Waiyaki tried to recover his breath. But he now felt foolish. What had he come to warn them against? What was he to tell these men of Joshua who sat around the table singing to heaven, waiting for a Christ?

'I am sorry for interrupting your meeting ... but ... but I think you are in danger. They may want to do something to you, tonight or another day.'

'Who?' several voices asked.

132

'Kabonyi and his men. The Kiama. I don't know what you can do but—'

'Do not tell us what we can do,' Joshua roared. He stood up and glared at Waiyaki. 'This is all lies.' The two men faced each other for the first time. The others watched, fascinated, fearing, wondering. 'Go! Go! Out of my house! So you would come back to entice the only daughter that is left to me. I have never forgotten what you did to Muthoni.'

It was the first time that Joshua had publicly mentioned her death.

Waiyaki felt hurt, as if this rejection of his well-meant warning had suddenly brought home to him the depth of the barrier between him and Joshua. Perhaps nothing would ever remove it. In that moment, too, he understood why Nyambura had refused him. Yet he felt himself ridiculed and humiliated before these people, before the girl he loved. He had seen Nyambura sitting beside Miriamu.

'Ni wega. I have done my duty. I was only trying to save you from danger.' His voice carried a slight tremor.

'Save yourself first. Save yourself from the Wrath to come. What do you, who have always worked against the people of God, want in my house?'

Waiyaki suddenly turned his back on them and opened the door to go out. The light from the house shone on him – a lone figure facing the darkness outside.

As Kamau and his four men, lurking in the outer darkness, saw him, they gasped with fear and unbelief. Kamau did not know that Waiyaki had gone so far in his betrayal of the people, and he became convinced that Waiyaki was the greatest enemy to the tribe. He could not now go to capture Nyambura as the Kiama had ordered them. No. He would go back and report this to the Kiama. This was no longer a personal battle, but a war between the tribe and Waiyaki.

Nyambura had seen Waiyaki's entrance. She read sorrow and agitation in his face. Her heart jumped with excitement. There stood her man. There stood Waiyaki, the Teacher, her

**133**

black Messiah, sent from heaven after Muthoni's death to come and rescue her from disintegration. And she knew the man loved her. She had heard it from his own lips. Since then she had thought about him day and night. It did not matter if her father forbade her standing with him. Joshua could control her body, but he could not control her heart. And so, day by day, she walked with him, touching him and holding him to herself in her own way. She lived in a dream. She was always with Waiyaki. Yet sometimes the separation pained her. It hurt her and at times made her cry. For she too yearned for him and wanted him to be near her all the time. She cried: 'Waiyaki, you are mine. Come back to me.' But he did not come. Her duty to her parents stood between him and her. A religion of love and forgiveness stood between them. No! It could never be a religion of love. Never, never. The religion of love was in the heart. The other was Joshua's own religion, which ran counter to her spirit and violated love. If the faith of Joshua and Livingstone came to separate, why, it was not good. If it came to stand between a father and his daughter so that her death did not move him, then it was inhuman. She wanted the other. The other that held together, the other that united. The voice that long ago said 'Come unto me all we that labour and are heavy laden, and I will give you rest' soothed her and she wanted to hear it again and again, as she lay near the Honia river and listened to the throb which echoed the secret beating of her heart. And she remembered:

The wolf also shall dwell with the lamb, and the leopard shall lie down with the kid; and the calf and the young lion and the fatling together; and a little child shall lead them. And the cow and the bear shall feed; their young ones shall lie down together: and the lion shall eat straw like the ox. And the sucking child shall play on the hole of the asp, and the weaned child shall put his hand on the cockatrice' den. They shall not hurt nor destroy in all my holy mountain: for the earth shall be full of the knowledge of the Lord, as the waters cover the sea.

134

That was her religion. That was what she now wanted for her tribe. It was the faith that would give life and peace to all. So she clung to this now as she prayed that Waiyaki would come back to her.

He came. Not when she expected him. But she was ready for him and she was glad. She, however, feared for him. Maybe that was why her heart jumped. That was why something strange settled in her bowels, giving her both pain and pleasure.

She looked at the two men standing face to face. She saw her Waiyaki being humiliated. Her obedience to her father fought with her love for Waiyaki. And at last, when he turned his back, rejected, she stood up. Her voice was clear and almost commanding.

'Teacher!' Waiyaki stopped.

'Come back!'

Waiyaki obeyed. Yet it was all like a dream. Even Joshua was shocked to silence. To think that she had actually called him the 'Teacher'.

'The teacher is not telling a lie.'

'You! You! How can you know that, little rebel?'

'I know. Last week Kamau wanted me to marry him. I refused. He said he would compel me or do something worse. He said I was in his power and he was the only person who could save—'

Joshua fumed with fury. He would not let her finish. And Waiyaki was still in a dream. But still he was hurt and a burning anger was urging him to go out. Outside he heard a faint noise. At first it had seemed distant but now he could hear some words – Teacher ... traitor. .... A heavy dejection came over Waiyaki. He knew now that he was not wanted by them in spite of all he had done for the hills. And the words of his father came back to him. *But they rejected Mugo,* his thin boy's voice had queried. *Let them do what they like. A time will come when they shall cry for a saviour.*

Had the time come? Was Kabonyi the saviour they were crying for? And what would Kabonyi do? He would only destroy what Waiyaki had built. But no. He could not. Surely there was a soul, a heart where at least what Waiyaki had done had taken root. And the teachers who were coming! They would carry on the work. The voices singing death became louder and louder. He thought they were coming towards Joshua's house. He went back to the hut to make one more desperate appeal.

'Be careful. They may be coming here.'

'Go, go out from here. Get thee behind me, Satan.'

Joshua was fierce. He hated the young man with the hatred which a man of God has towards Satan. There was another murmur in the room. Then silence reigned as Nyambura walked across towards Waiyaki while all the eyes watched her. Waiyaki and Joshua must have both been struck by her grace and mature youthfulness. She held Waiyaki's hand and said what no other girl at that time would have dared to say, what she herself could not have done a few days before.

'You are brave and I love you.'

Joshua woke up from his stupor. He would never have thought that this meek, quiet and obedient daughter could be capable of such an action. He rushed towards her and was about to lay his hands on her when he realized that this was another temptation brought to him by Satan. Christ in him must triumph at this hour of trial. Waiyaki and Nyambura were standing near the door.

'For me and my house we will serve the Lord,' Joshua declared, pointing at Nyambura with the forefinger of his right hand. 'You are not my daughter. Yet let me warn you,' he continued, his voice changing from one of fiery anger to one of calm sorrow, 'you will come to an untimely end. Go!'

As if in a dream, Waiyaki and Nyambura went out. Miriamu was weeping and saying, 'Don't let her go. Don't,' while the others remained silent, wondering what curse had befallen Joshua's house.

Darkness still blanketed the land. Above the stars had gone out except for one or two. Nyambura had never rebelled before; not with deliberation. This was her first act of rebellion and she now knew that she was beyond the grasp of

Joshua. The call of the inner voice that urged her on, the call of the land beyond Joshua's confining hand, was too strong.

'Please, Nyambura. Go back to your father,' Waiyaki pleaded as soon as they had gone a few yards from the house and they were swallowed by the darkness. But she would not. And the voices that denounced him as a traitor rang through the darkness. Waiyaki remembered what Kinuthia had told him. And then it came – at first a small urge, but then it became stronger and stronger so that there was a real struggle in Waiyaki's soul. The insistent voice inside him told him to run and go to Nairobi. You have now the object of your heart's desire, and they have rejected you. Run! Run to Nairobi and live there happily with Nyambura. And why not? Had he not brought light to the hills, awakening the sleeping lions so that now they could shout 'Traitor'? Then he felt ashamed of himself. He could not run away. His father's words again glowed before him: '. . . salvation shall come from the hills. A man must rise and save the people in their hour of need. He shall show them the way; he shall lead them. . . .'

Waiyaki and Nyambura now stood on a piece of raised ground overlooking Honia Valley. They were near Kabonyi's house and that was where the voices came from. He felt frightened and his resolution not to run away wavered. He turned to the girl beside him and in a subdued voice said, 'Death awaits you there.'

She took his hand and pressed it slightly. Waiyaki's blood warmed and he felt as if he would be carried away by the waves of desire and emotion that shook his whole being.

'Oh, Teacher. I have always loved you. I'll go where you go. Don't leave me now.'

Waiyaki held her against his breast. Then they slowly descended the Makuyu ridge till they came to their sacred ground.

'Let's sit down,' he whispered. They lay on the grass and the Honia river went on with its throb. Waiyaki and Nyambura did not hear it, for a stronger throb, heart-rending, was sweeping away their bodies. Their souls joined into one stillness; so still that their breathing seemed to belong to another world, apart from them.

When they rose to go a new strength had come to Waiyaki. Even Kinuthia, who had gone back to wait for him in the hut, was surprised more at the brightness on their faces than at the fact of their being together. Indeed Waiyaki felt his yearning soul soothed by the healing presence of this girl. Yet he knew that he would be forced to make a choice, a choice between the girl and the tribe. Tonight he felt he had something to say to the people. But he did not know what. He wanted a rest; time to make a silent inquiry into his heart. His father's image came back to him vividly. He remembered that journey into the sacred grove. And he said loudly, 'I shall go there tomorrow.'

'Where?' Kinuthia asked.

Waiyaki was shaken into the present by that question. He felt he could not explain his journey even to Kinuthia. Yet just now he felt his father's presence everywhere in the room, in the darkness outside. This feeling was as real to him as the presence of Nyambura, who had fallen asleep on his bed. She was very exhausted but she felt at peace.

'To the hill south of Kameno. To the sacred grove.'

'To the sacred grove?'

'Yes, it is a long story.' And now he told Kinuthia about it all, the journey with his father, the ancient prophecy and his bewilderment at its meaning. And Kinuthia sat mouth open; a new veneration for Waiyaki grew upon him. It was as if Waiyaki was a revelation, a thing not of this earth.

'Look here, Kinuthia,' Waiyaki said after a long silence. 'Do something for me. Tomorrow I must speak to the people just before the sunset. Call a meeting at Honia river on the initiation ground. It is flat there. Get some people to help you spread the news. On every hill. I'll fight it out with Kabonyi in the open. For, Kinuthia, I cannot run away. New thoughts are coming into my mind. Things I might have done and said. Oh, there are so many things I did not know. I had not seen that the new awareness wanted expression at a political level. Education for an oppressed people is not all. But I must think. I must be alone.'

Still they talked far into the night and Kinuthia listened to Waiyaki's plans and felt himself inspired to new efforts and transported to new heights.

'I will never leave you!' he cried. 'Whatever the others do, I will be with you all the way.'

'Thank you, Kinuthia. Let us wait until tomorrow.'

# CHAPTER TWENTY-FIVE

He felt a dull pain inside his heart. He was weary. The country was below him again, but it did not have so much power over him as when he had stood there, a child, with his father. The sun was up and he could not see Kerinyaga. And the sacred grove seemed to be no more than ordinary bush clustering around the fig tree. But there was something strange about the tree. It was still huge and there was a firmness about it that would for ever defy time; that indeed seemed to scorn changing weather. And Waiyaki wondered how many people before him had stood there, where he now was, how many had indeed come to pay homage to this tree, the symbol of a people's faith in a mysterious power ruling the universe and the destinies of men.

And now he felt that mystery gradually enveloping him. But for him now the mystery was that of darkness clouding his heart. That was where in his loneliness he struggled with strange forces, forces that seemed to be destroying him. He wondered why he had come here. He wondered what answers he had hoped to find to the unformulated questions in his mind. Even Nyambura had faded from the reality around him and was no longer a consolation. For the reality around him, around his heart, was one of despair because he was aware that he was fighting against forces that he himself did not understand; forces that he had felt in the air all over the country. And he was afraid. Perhaps he was running away from what he did not understand because he feared. What had he awakened in the hills? And he remembered Kinuthia telling him: Your name will be your ruin.

Waiyaki stared at the country below him as if he were seeing nothing. Below the calm of the hills were strange stirrings.

What had brought all this trouble? Waiyaki blamed himself.

He felt that things had really begun to go wrong from the time of the great meeting, the time when they all declared him the Teacher. Since then the rifts between the various factions had widened and the attempt by the Kiama to burn people's houses and their threat to Joshua and his followers were all an expression of that widened gulf. Perhaps he should not have resigned from the Kiama, he told himself over and over again. What if he had made his stand clear at that meeting? That was now a lost opportunity and he had to reckon with the present. Still he wondered if he had not betrayed the tribe; the tribe he had meant to unite; the tribe he had wanted to save; the people he had wanted to educate, giving them all the benefits of the white man's coming.

For Waiyaki knew that not all the ways of the white man were bad. Even his religion was not essentially bad. Some good, some truth shone through it. But the religion, the faith, needed washing, cleaning away all the dirt, leaving only the eternal. And that eternal that was the truth had to be reconciled to the traditions of the people. A people's traditions could not be swept away overnight. That way lay disintegration. Such a tribe would have no roots, for a people's roots were in their traditions going back to the past, the very beginning, Gikuyu and Mumbi. A religion that took no count of people's way of life, a religion that did not recognize spots of beauty and truths in their way of life, was useless. It would not satisfy. It would not be a living experience, a source of life and vitality. It would only maim a man's soul, making him fanatically cling to whatever promised security, otherwise he would be lost. Perhaps that was what was wrong with Joshua. He had clothed himself with a religion decorated and smeared with everything *white*. He renounced his past and cut himself away from those life-giving traditions of the tribe. And because he had nothing to rest upon, something rich and firm on which to stand and grow, he had to cling with his hands to whatever the missionaries taught him promised future.

Waiyaki wondered if he himself fitted anywhere. Did Kabonyi? Which of the two was the messiah, the man who was to bring hope in salvation to a troubled people? But how could a man be a saviour when he himself had already lost that contact with the past?

Muthoni had tried. Hers was a search for salvation for herself. She had the courage to attempt a reconciliation of the many forces that wanted to control her. She had realized her need, the need to have a wholesome and beautiful life that enriched you and made you grow. His father, too, had tried to reconcile the two ways, not in himself, but through his son. Waiyaki was a product of that attempt. Yes, in the quietness of the hill, Waiyaki had realized many things. Circumcision of women was not important as a physical operation. It was what it did inside a person. It could not be stopped overnight. Patience and, above all, education, were needed. If the white man's religion made you abandon a custom and then did not give you something else of equal value, you became lost. An attempt at resolution of the conflict would only kill you, as it did Muthoni.

Waiyaki now thought it was time to go. The sacred grove had not lit the way for him. He did not quite know where he was going or what he really wanted to tell his people. He was still in the dark. He remembered Nyambura and wondered how she was feeling, being in his hut. For a moment he was gripped by terror and hated himself for having left the hut. What if they had come and taken her by force? What if Joshua had gone to report him at the Government Post? He again wondered if he should not run away and, as he descended the hill, he cast his eyes beyond. He had a vision of many possibilities and opportunities there, away from the hills. Maybe one day he would go there. Maybe one day he would join forces with the men from Muranga, Kiambu and Nyeri and with one voice tell the white man 'Go!' And all at once Waiyaki realized what the ridges wanted. All at once he felt more forcefully than he had ever felt before the shame of a people's land being taken away, the shame of being forced to work on those same lands, the humiliation of paying taxes for a government that you knew nothing about.

Yes. The Kiama was right. People wanted action now. The stirrings in the hills were an awakening to the shame and humiliation of their condition. Their isolation had been violated. But what action was needed? What had he to do now? How could he organize people into a political organization when they were so torn with strife and disunity? Now he knew what he would preach if he ever got another chance: education for unity. Unity for political freedom. For a time this vision made his heart glow with expectation and new hope. He quickened his descent, wishing to come to the people and communicate this new vision. Education, Unity, Political Freedom. And then came the doubt. What if they should ask him to give up Nyambura? What if – he did not want to think about it. He would fight for unity and Nyambura was an integral part of that battle. If he lost Nyambura, he too would be lost. He was fighting for his salvation.

Many people had come to the meeting ground. There were women and children and old men who were bewildered by the urgent call they had received from Kinuthia's messengers. And they came because they wanted to hear what their Teacher had to say and because they had heard things which they could not believe. Most still clung to the vision of the Teacher they knew; the Teacher whom they trusted, in whom they believed, a man they could always follow, anywhere. How could they believe that he would betray them? How could they believe this story about his marrying an uncircumcised girl, a daughter of Joshua, the enemy of the people? Waiyaki had awakened them to new visions, new desires, new aspirations. He had restored to them their dignity as a tribe and he had given them the white man's education when the missionaries had wanted to deny them that wisdom. Waiyaki had been too clever for them. He had taken the oath of loyalty to the purity of the tribe. That had been an example to all. Could he then go against the oath, could he?

They waited patiently, the sun's heat on their bare heads; sweat rolled down their backs. And still they waited. And

Kabonyi was there and the elders of the Kiama and the young men of the tribe. And all waited, waited for Waiyaki to come. They nursed their secret thoughts to their hearts and they looked forward to his arrival and they knew that this was the day of trial. Initiation day would be tomorrow on this very ground and tonight would be the night of singing and dancing. Joshua and his followers would sing tonight for their Christ was going to be born tonight. But at the meeting nobody sung, nobody danced. They waited to hear what their Teacher would say.

And Kabonyi and some of the elders sat in a group separately and trembled with their secret knowledge. Let the people wait. Kabonyi was determined to win or die. For he knew that his victory was the victory of the tribe; that tribe that was now threatened by Waiyaki. And he hated Waiyaki intensely and identified this hatred with the wrath of the tribe against impurity and betrayal. To him then, this was not a personal struggle. It was a continuation of that struggle that had always existed between Makuyu and Kameno. For leaders from Kameno had failed; they had only betrayed people. The ridges would now rise and cry vengeance. Kabonyi felt himself the instrument of that vengeance. He was the saviour for whom the people waited. Not that Kabonyi knew exactly where he would lead the people. For he too was grappling with forces awakened in the people. How could he understand that the people did not want to move backwards, that the ridges no longer desired their isolation? How could he know that the forces that drove people to yearn for a better day tomorrow, that now gave a new awareness to the people, were like demons, sweeping the whole country, as Mugo had said, from one horizon touching the sea to the other horizon touching the water?

The sun was going down and people stirred with impatience. Some people, among whom were a group of Joshua's followers, stood on the hill. They had not yet descended. Miriamu was there. She too thought something was going to happen and she wept for her daughter; and she wept too because she knew she was weak and she could not do anything. And suddenly the people who stood on the hills or up the slope saw big yellow flames emanated by the setting sun. The flames seemed near and far and the trees and the country were caught in the flames. They feared.

Kinuthia too feared and for a time he had a momentary glimpse of Waiyaki and Nyambura caught in those flames. And he cried and blamed himself because he had failed Waiyaki. Nyambura had been stolen from Waiyaki's hut and he knew that she was in the hands of Kabonyi and the Kiama. How could he communicate this to Waiyaki? How would Waiyaki take it? He decided to let Waiyaki face the crowd and fight the battle unhampered by his fear for Nyambura. Then from somewhere people began to sing: 'He has gone – traitor.' Kinuthia trembled and wondered if Waiyaki would not turn up. If he did not, then Kinuthia's life would be in danger, for the people's wrath would turn against him. He sweated with fear as the people cried 'Seek him out.' It was Kabonyi and his followers who were shouting 'traitor'.

The crowd was big and more people were coming. Then there was a whisper which made everybody rise in excitement: 'The Teacher! The Teacher!' Then they sat down again and let Waiyaki pass, his head and broad shoulders indeed caught against the yellow beams that passed through the trees. And he looked powerful and beautiful and they were tense on both sides of the Honia river. Great hush fell over the land as he strode towards a raised piece of ground where the Kiama sat, where his destiny would be decided.

# CHAPTER TWENTY-SIX

Even Waiyaki was affected by that great hush that fell over the land. He could hear his heart beat and he told himself: I must not fear. And he stood at a raised piece of ground and looked at the people; at their expectant faces and eyes. *Salvation shall come from the hills.* And he saw that many people had come and had filled up the initiation ground and the slopes of the hills. Some had climbed up trees. *A man shall rise and save the people in their hour of need.* And he remembered his father, and Mugo wa Kibiro, Wachiori, Kamiri, Gikuyu and Mumbi. And he remembered Kerinyaga as he had seen it that great day with his father. *I will look up into the hills from whence cometh my help.* Waiyaki prayed that the cold fear that settled in his stomach be removed. Kameno and Makuyu seemed to be staring at him ready to pounce on him. *He shall show them the way; he shall lead them.*

Waiyaki realized all too suddenly that this was the hour, the great hour of need. The tribe needed him now. Nyambura needed him now. And he needed himself too. Kabonyi was a destructive element. He did not know the way. But Waiyaki was ready, there to move together with the people, to grope in the dark maybe, but together, searching for the light, looking for the way. And he remembered this was the piece of ground on which he had shed his blood; that too had been an oath. And he was now prepared to defend that soil.

He began to speak. At first he made a small speech; thanked the people for coming; asked them to bear with him. He had been stunned by the recent development in the hills: hatred and rivalry such as would destroy the people. He outlined his struggles in the service of the people, especially in the now ending year; it was the year that saw the transformation of the hills, a year that had awakened the sleeping lions. He told them of his attempts to get more teachers. He had succeeded although it was a difficult task. But when he came back he was accused by the Kiama of being a traitor. Some people, he said, had gone out at night and were singing that he was a traitor. Let those people now stand in front and accuse him publicly. If he had wronged the ridges, people would know what to do with him.

A big roar of 'The Teacher' greeted his brief speech. Some cried 'The Teacher is right,' though they did not know what he was right about. Others cried 'Let Kabonyi come forward.' And Kabonyi stood up with dignity. Their unfinished battle was now on.

He was once a Joshua follower. Now he was the Leader of the Kiama and he lived in Makuyu. He spoke with the authority of a man who knows the secret workings, evil and good, in men's hearts and in the country. His big accusation was that Waiyaki was unclean. He had *thahu* and if he continued teaching the people there would be darkness instead of light. When a girl called Muthoni died because she was visited by evil spirits, Waiyaki had taken her to the white man's hospital in Siriana, and was never cleansed. As he was a leader, his *thahu* had visited the tribe. It was now for the tribe to take action. For Waiyaki was a greater menace than the people realized. He was in league with the white man, who had brought a secret religion to quieten the people while the land was being grabbed by their brothers. And taxation? Who did not now complain of the heavy taxation imposed on the men and women? He described Waiyaki's many secret journeys to Siriana under the pretext of getting more teachers for the people. When the Kiama said that people should take arms against the Government Post (it was very small anyway, it would not be difficult to take it) Waiyaki opposed this and cried: 'Education! Education!' Will education give us back our land? Let him answer that.

He sat down. Waiyaki noticed that Kabonyi had carefully avoided any mention of Joshua or Nyambura. Why? He thought that he too would avoid dragging in the name of

Nyambura but he would speak of unity. Now, or he would never get another chance.

Kabonyi's speech had been greeted first with stony silence and then with murmuring. The sun was slowly going down.

Waiyaki's voice was calm and compelling. His eyes shone and anger began to stir in him, for now he knew without any doubt that Kabonyi was determined to see his ruin.

'What does Kabonyi want?' he asked. 'Who first followed the white man and embraced the new faith? Who betrayed the tribe when Makuyu and Kameno and the other ridges could have risen in arms against the white man?'

He turned to the people and in simple words reminded them of their history. 'It was before Agu and Agu, at the beginning of things, that Murungu, the Creator, gave rise to Gikuyu and Mumbi, father and mother of the tribe. He made them stand on the holy ground on top of Kerinyaga and showed them all the land. You remember what he told them; the great Promise that he gave to our ancestors! "This land I give to you, O man and woman. It is yours to till, you and your posterity." The land was fertile and in it grew all the fruit, and honey was there in plenty. When he brought them to Kameno, they still saw the land was beautiful. They were happy and with content in their hearts followed Murungu to Mukuruwe wa Gathanga, where he kept them. And now we who are the descendants of the nine daughters of Gikuyu and Mumbi are torn with strife and rivalry.'

He spoke of the great heroes of the tribe and mentioned Demi na Mathathi, Wachiori, Mugo wa Kibiro and Kamiri. He told them of the great victories that these heroes had over the Masai and other enemy tribes.

'It is because the hills were united that such great victories were possible. People stood together in the hour of need, giving one another the warmth of their contact, the strength of their blood.'

He told them about Mugo wa Kibiro and his prophecy that there would come a people with clothes like butterflies.

'But people rejected him. And when the white man came, jealousy stood between Kameno and Makuyu. You would not come together. And you left the white man alone. Now, instead of learning his ways and coming together so that united we may drive him out, Kabonyi and a few others cry for vengeance against Joshua and his followers. That is what I have come to tell you today. We are all children of Mumbi and we must fight together in one political movement, or else we perish and the white man will always be on our back. Can a house divided against itself stand?'

'No-o-o,' they roared in unison.

'Then we must stand together. We must end the ancient rivalry.'

People seemed moved, and when he sat down they rose and, as if of one voice, shouted: 'The Teacher! The Teacher!' And when Kabonyi stood to speak, people began to press towards Kabonyi as if animated with the desire to tear him into pieces. And they would have done it and that might have been the end of threats to their teacher, but for Waiyaki, who stopped the crowd. 'No! No!' he shouted. 'Do not touch him.' It was as if Waiyaki at that moment realized that Kabonyi and the Kiama were also in their way an expression of something felt and desired by the tribe.

They listened to their Teacher, their saviour, as if they would say, We shall never give you up. And Kinuthia thought of moving forward and giving a warning to Waiyaki, but a big fear settled on him, weakening his knees so that he did not move from where he sat. Instead he sought to hide himself in the crowd as if he did not want to be identified with the Teacher. As for Waiyaki, he was amazed because he did not know that he had such power over the people.

He could not even listen to what Kabonyi was saying about the break with the missions, and about purity. It was only when Kabonyi mentioned something about the oath that Waiyaki grew attentive. And he found that every other person was attentive to Kabonyi, who now spoke with a broken voice, full of grief. To break oath was one of the most serious crimes that a man could commit. Such a person was doomed to destruction.

People knew that Waiyaki had taken an oath given by Kiama never to contaminate the tribe with impurity and never to reveal the secrets of the Kiama, secrets which involved the political destiny of the hills. So when Kabonyi said that Waiyaki had broken that oath people roared back 'No-o-o.' How could they believe it? How could they believe that Waiyaki was in league with Joshua for the destruction of the ridges? They again shouted 'No-o-o!' Waiyaki remembered Nyambura at home and he felt afraid. He wanted to go back to his hut and see if she was safe. Then he wondered about Kinuthia. He had not seen him at the meeting. Maybe he was with Nyambura. He felt relieved and heard Kabonyi's next words.

'I can prove to you, beyond any doubts, that he is a Joshua's man in spite of his oath.'

They cried 'Prove! Prove!' He waited for the confusion to die and then said, 'He is marrying his daughter.' Another hush fell over the land before there were cries of 'No! Not the Teacher,' and Waiyaki trembled slightly and he waited fearing, yet did not know what he feared. He wanted to rise and speak to the people and tell them about Nyambura and how he had gone to rescue her, but his knees failed him as he saw Nyambura in the gathering twilight, brought by Kamau and two other young men. She was made to stand before the people.

'Let him deny her.' Kabonyi threw the challenge, which went bouncing on people's ears to Makuyu and Kameno, to the trees that patiently waited and to the birds that did not make any noise. And Honia river went on flowing through the valley of life, throbbing, murmuring an unknown song.

*They shall not hurt nor destroy in all my holy mountains, for the earth shall be full of the knowledge of the Lord, as the waters cover the sea.*

And the people shouted 'The oath! The oath!' as if they were warning their Teacher. Waiyaki stood up and his eyes met

**150**

those of Nyambura. And he remembered her on this very ground that time she was praying alone; it was the day he first held her in his arms. And she looked beautiful now. She looked like a lamb on the altar of sacrifice. And Waiyaki knew that he could not deny her now, that he could not go back on his love for her.

There was a long silence. People held their breath. Waiyaki thought of making a speech. Then the thought went bouncing away and instead he could only hear the challenge of Kabonyi. How could he deny her now? How . . . ? He took her arms and the silence that followed was oppressive. And Nyambura felt a warmth and an assurance that drove away her doubts; they compensated her for the suffering of the day. How could she have doubted the Teacher? Even Waiyaki felt a new strength which drove away the bitter thoughts of why he had taken the oath. Yet the oath did not say that he should not love. And that was what he wanted to tell the people. But as he tried to open his mouth, one woman screamed 'The oath!' and the cry was taken over by the other people as an outlet to the oppressive feelings that burdened them. How could their Teacher betray them? How could he work for the togetherness and purity of the tribe and then marry a girl who was not circumcised? How could he do this to them?

Waiyaki tried to silence them but they would not listen. They only cried 'The oath' and their cry was echoed in the forest. And how could he tell them now that he had not betrayed them, but this was not what he meant by unity; that he was not in league with Joshua? How could he tell them that he meant to serve the hills; that he meant to lead them into a political movement that would shake the whole country, that would tell the white man 'Go!' He looked beyond and saw the children he had helped in their thirst for learning; the teachers who were coming; Kinuthia . . . and he wondered 'Where is Kinuthia?' And then in doubt, a doubt that shocked him into a few minutes of agonized silence. Had Kinuthia betrayed him? Had Kinuthia been in league with Kabonyi?

An elder stood up. Waiyaki could not hear what he was

saying for his mind was full of many thoughts and doubts that came and went. Waiyaki and Nyambura would be placed in the hands of the Kiama, who would judge them and decide what to do. It was the best thing and the crowd roared back 'Yes' as if the burden of judging their Teacher were removed from them. They went away quickly, glad that he was hidden by the darkness. For they did not want to look at the Teacher and they did not want to read their guilt in one another's faces. Neither did they want to speak to one another, for they knew full well what they had done to Waiyaki and yet they did not want to know.

The land was now silent. The two ridges lay side by side, hidden in the darkness. And Honia river went on flowing between them, down through the valley of life, its beat rising above the dark stillness, reaching into the heart of the people of Makuyu and Kameno.

# THE AFRICAN WRITERS SERIES

## KAREN KING-ARIBISALA
### Kicking Tongues

*Kicking Tongues* brilliantly transposes Chaucer's *Canterbury Tales* to modern-day Nigeria. Forty travellers gather at the Eko Holiday Inn, Lagos, intending to journey to Abuja, the new federal capital. They are united only by their dissatisfaction with Nigeria's chaotic and corrupt regime, a concern which is reflected in the widely differing stories they tell on the journey.

## NADINE GORDIMER
### Crimes of Conscience

A selection of short stories which vividly describe human conditions and the turmoil of a violent world outside the individual incidents, where the instability of fear and uncertainty lead unwittingly to crimes of conscience.

## NGŨGĨ
### Matigari

This is a moral fable telling the story of a freedom fighter and his quest for Truth and Justice. It is set in the political dawn of post-independence Kenya.
'Clear, subtle, mischievous, passionate novel' *Sunday Times*

## AMECHI AKWANYA
### Orimili

Set in a complex Nigerian community that's at the point of irrevocable change, this is the story of a man's struggle to be accepted in the company of his town's elders.

## SHIMMER CHINODYA
### Harvest of Thorns

'Zimbabwe has fine black writers and Shimmer Chinodya is one of the best. *Harvest of Thorns* brilliantly pictures the transition between the old, white-dominated Southern Rhodesia, through the Bush War, to the new black regime. It is a brave book, a good strong story, and it is often very funny. People who know the country will salute its honesty, but I hope newcomers to African writing will give this book a try. They won't be disappointed.' Doris Lessing

## CHINUA ACHEBE
### Things Fall Apart

This, the first title in the African Writers Series, describes how a man in the Igbo tribe of Nigeria became exiled from the tribe and returned only to be forced to commit suicide to escape the results of his rash courage against the white man.

## STEVE BIKO
### I Write What I Like

'An impressive tribute to the depth and range of his thought, covering such diverse issues as the basic philosophy of black consciousness, Bantustans, African culture, the institutional church, and Western involvement in apartheid.'
*The Catholic Herald*